Praise for *Cracking the College Financial Code*

Stan Targosz and Will Alford truly have "cracked the code" to college financial planning in this important book. Those who read it not only will gain insight about college affordability, but also position themselves, family members, and friends for choosing a school that represents the best path for success, regardless of tuition price. In making one of the most important decisions of your life, that is priceless knowledge.

Robert P. Bartlett, Ph.D.,
President
Michigan Colleges Alliance

Planning for college is a critical element of financial planning—and it is most definitely not a D-I-Y (do-it-yourself) project. Why?

- First, huge money is on the line. Most people grossly underestimate how much help is out there.

- Second, many people operate under the misconception that they have too much, make too much, or their student isn't exceptional enough to qualify for much assistance. They're usually wrong–in a good way.

- Third, college planning is highly complex - the rules are obscure—solid, reliable information is hard to come by—and few financial advisors have the information and experience you really need.

- Fourth, college comes at a time in parents' lives when the most money will be flowing out of their family economy. But it is also the time in life that is most critical to setting up a great retirement. Failing to professionally prepare for college too often results in sacrificing retirement dreams for college hopes—and it's completely unnecessary.

If I knew personally what Stan and Will teach when my kids were going through college, I'd have nearly a quarter million more dollars at retirement. One can't make many quarter-million dollar mistakes in a lifetime and come out on the right end of financial success.

James L (Jay) Beattey, IV
Chief Executive Officer
Velomon Group

Cracking the College Financial Code

Every Family has a Different Combination:
Learn How to Unlock Yours

Stan Targosz and Will Alford

Thought Leadership Publishing

Permissions@ThoughtLeadershipPublishing.com

Ordering Information:

Quantity sales: Special discounts are available on quantity purchases by corporations, associations, and others. For details, contact the "Special Sales Department" at Orders@ThoughtLeadershipPublishing.com

Cracking the College Financial Code/Stan Targosz and Will Alford. — 1st ed.

ISBN-13: 978-0-692-66549-7
ISBN-10: 0-692-66549-8

Contents

Foreward

How many times have you looked back in your life and said, "I wish I knew about that 20 years ago? I would have saved so much money, made more money or I would be healthier."

Stan and Will's book will help eliminate that statement from a college perspective. They have heard hundreds of horror stories from families who have done everything from a traditional planning perspective and ended up overpaying for their children's education.

Student, and especially parent loans, are among the largest growing areas of debt in our country. However, there is hope. There are sound strategies available that will help keep you in control of the cost of college and reduce the amount of debt your family will have upon graduation.

Stan and Will have helped families save millions of dollars on their out-of-pocket cost for college. Millions of dollars more have been reduced in student and parent loans by using this information. This book will have you thinking differently about college and the opportunities that your child has, while opening doors and allowing you to sleep at night knowing that you are finally in control.

James L (Jay) Beattey, IV
Chief Executive Officer
Velomon Group

Acknowledgements

Stan Targosz

I owe a lot of credit for this book and all projects that I have been a part of to God. Without His guidance and support, none of this would be possible. The second most important person in this whole process is my wife, Colleen. She has been a stable rock, encouraging me and supporting me during the good times and the tough ones. She has been able to withstand the long process to accomplish this as well as many other projects in which I am involved. It takes a lot of energy to support our family and let me follow my passions. My children Selah, Stas', and Gabrielle have been patient with my schedule and allowed me to do what it takes to make an impact in the community and take time away from them to accomplish this goal. They have always been loving and welcoming every time I see them. It is so satisfying to have my kids see me work toward something I believe in.

My parents, Stan Jr. and Mary, and my brother Adam and sister Lori ask about my business and always let me know they are proud of me just when I need it most. There are many team members who have been with us from the very start and new people who have helped us refine our process and become better. To mention names would require an additional book.

Finally, Will Alford is the glue that holds our company and this project together. I have been overwhelming at times and very persistent, sometimes without regard to other issues, and he has always been able to take my mediocre work and turn it into something great. Without his final touches on this and everything else, I would not have any complete projects. Instead, I would own a thousand half-started ideas. It takes a team, and I am so grateful to have found the best teammates at home and in business.

Will Alford

Stan Targosz and I started Education Planning Resources in 2008 with a simple idea of helping parents find a way to pay for college without going into inescapable debt. What started out as a simple idea to help families pay for college quickly morphed into a crusade to change lives.

When Stan approached me with the idea to write a book on college, I was intrigued. As I do with most of the ideas he has, I eagerly agreed to the proposition, only later to amuse myself with just how ambitious the project would be. As with anyone who has ever made the decision to publish a book, I never envisioned how difficult it would be. Even after thousands of edits, the process never seems to end. But it finally did, and I hope the information provided in this book continues our quest to change lives for the better.

Were it not for the infinite patience and understanding of my wife Karen, I would never have been able to finish this book. She is my soul mate, and I thank her for supporting me while not only working on this book, but also running a thriving business at the same time. My children Austin, Kevin and Ella provide inspiration and light up each and every day of my life.

Thanks go to my brothers, Rick and Paul, for including me in your lives when I was younger, even though you were much older than I. Although I knew you let me score all those touchdowns in sandlot football with your much bigger and faster friends, I didn't care. I always looked up to you both, and I thank you for providing me a set of life standards to aspire to.

I must also thank my mother, Caroline, for instilling such a can-do attitude in me during my formative years. Her endless encouragement during my childhood has provided me a belief that I can do anything I set my mind to. If you have a goal in mind, never give up until the goal becomes a reality. Failure exists only as a stepping stone to success.

A few other people also deserve mention. I must thank Jay Beattey, a successful author in his own right, for reviewing the first draft and providing valuable insight in structuring the ebb and flow of topics throughout the book. Marge Wisniewski helped me clean up myriad grammar and sentence structure problems. Who knew it could be possible to find so many errors after the eighth revision of the book? I cannot forget the support of the team we have in our business. I have never been a part of a group that acts so selflessly, working tirelessly to support our vision and the thousands of families we have been blessed to be able to impact in such powerful ways.

Of course, where would I be without the wizard behind the curtain, Stan Targosz? There is not a week that goes by where I am not astounded by yet another brilliant idea. As crazy as some of his ideas appear, most of them come true. Stan provides the vision while I do my best to make those visions a reality. Along the way we have become the best of friends, and I have an undying tide of respect for his ability to stay the course.

Finally, I must thank God for always being there for me, even more so during the challenging times than the triumphant times. Without Him, nothing is possible.

Preface

The most important reason Will and I are in this business is to develop leaders in every community and in your family to help with college. We believe that we can change the landscape of America, one family at a time. Each time we save a family $50,000-$250,000 in student/parent loans we are setting them up to achieve their dreams and start their lives out on the right foot. By reducing the amount of student and parent debt, Will and I are helping families retire earlier and at a higher standard of living; college graduates are able to get married and buy houses sooner; graduates are able to choose jobs that are satisfying and fulfilling instead of based on income. Most important, people across the country are less enslaved to insurmountable college debt!

As I began my journey in this great industry of traditional financial planning, I had the privilege of learning from an out-of-the-box thinker who is an industry hero. Leonard Renier, founder of Wealth & Wisdom Institute, invited me into his business to work with clients and other financial professionals from around the country. We helped families learn about future taxes and strategies that positively impact individuals instead of only benefitting Uncle Sam or Wall Street.

I actually fell in love with Len's daughter, Colleen, married her, and then found my life's passion through working with Len. Len has a tremendous knack for communicating difficult subjects and making them appear simple to understand.

Wealth & Wisdom is an educational institute that shares how money truly works and how we can expect taxes, the government and the demographics of our country to impact our ability to save and weather the storm of retirement. I quickly learned that Len had something special going on and that he was getting the attention of the best of the best. He has written several books, including *How to Avoid Unintended Consequences* and *Sudden Impact*, both of which are best sellers.

Len Renier is an expert on the demographics of this country and has studied other masterminds such as David Walker, former Comptroller General of the United States. Len is making a difference wherever he goes, by educating financial advisors and families on how money works.

As Len was investing time training me, I had the opportunity to attend his speaking engagements and hear his message repeatedly. I spent the first six years working side by side with him, soaking up as much of the information as I could.

When Len was speaking, I had the opportunity to pick the brains of the top financial advisors everywhere we went. They thought differently than the average advisor and had solutions that the average person could have easily understood and implemented, but had not previously done so because they were uninformed. I needed to know more, so I spent many years learning his methods and message.

The concepts I learned from Len that had the biggest impact on my career were simple to understand and easy to implement. Unlike the traditional financial world, they did not use a product at the center of the solution. Instead, they used a thought process. This creates a paradigm shift in the way people think about money, and my goal is that by the time you finish reading this book, you will think differently about college and money.

Stan Targosz

Introduction

There are almost four thousand colleges and universities in this country. Each one specializes in something different from the others. Each one has a different formula to determine what your family will pay for your child to attend. This book will guide you through the process and open many doors that you thought were closed forever because of cost. Once the college game is understood, your family can make educated decisions on the best college for your child based on facts instead of the fear of an unrealistic sticker price or the concern of having $100,000 in student debt. Implementing the correct strategies will help you avoid trapping your child for years and limiting him or her from experiencing a successful life after college.

As you explore this book, you will see how to reduce your FAFSA score, how the FAFSA Expected Family Contribution can impact your cost of college, and how important it is to find high gifting colleges and universities. This new knowledge will assist you in designing a strategy to pay for college, keeping your family at the center of the process instead of Sallie Mae, FAFSA, Uncle Sam or the banks.

Who Should Read This Book

This book is designed as a guide for parents, grandparents or anyone who is directly involved in helping to pay for college. It is meant to challenge the traditional, often outdated, thought process surrounding college planning and help you design a plan that will work in today's ever-changing college environment. Those who have a desire to educate themselves on the most cutting-edge information and strategies should enjoy this book.

This college process is a missing link in the traditional financial world. This missing link connects the hard work families put in early in their family history with what they can expect to get out later in retirement. Many families are on track with their planning from a traditional perspective, yet when their kids reach college, they see all the hard work go right out the window. Paying for college ultimately leads to more debt, longer working careers, less savings, less retirement and most importantly, a constant struggle to attain their desired lifestyle during retirement. College has a bigger impact on the rest of your life than it ever has. This book is designed to help you preserve what you have worked hard for, provide strategies to keep your lifestyle in retirement intact, and control the process from start to finish.

About Us

We have been in the Financial Services industry since 2002. We started Education Planning Resources (EPR) in 2008 because we were meeting many families who were struggling to pay for college.

When we first started EPR, we were helping families find ways to pay for private grade school and high school tuition. We worked with several private high schools, helping parents find ways to pay for the jump in tuition from grade school to high school. Tuition at many of these schools increased from $3,000 or $4,000 per year in grade school to $10,000 or $12,000 per year in high school.

We found that parents were struggling to pay for high school, and they didn't have a plan for college. They were being forced into making a choice between continuing the private school education or being able to "somewhat" afford college.

We also found that most schools and parents did not understand the college process or how anyone should be expected to pay for it unless they were ultra-wealthy. These experiences inspired us to embark on a lifelong journey that has grown into both a passion and a business.

We have a weekly live radio show, <u>The College Connection</u>, which is broadcast on WMUZ-FM in Detroit. Visit our website at www.EducationPlanningResources.com for the most current information, live streaming or podcasts.

The expertise we have developed in the college planning arena has led us to the opportunity to train college planners across the country to guide parents with the most up-to-date strategies and solutions. Our business team is helping to make a tremendous difference as we guide families on how to best deal with the challenges of providing and paying for a college education.

EPR has gathered the best information and strategies and put them together in this book, with a goal of helping all parents who are worried about how they are going to afford their children's education. Finally, help and solutions are here.

Setting the Foundation

Before we get started, you should familiarize yourself with some basic terms, or college language. These will get you started:

<u>FAFSA</u> – Free Application for Federal Student Aid. The FAFSA is the financial aid form that must be completed each year someone is

attending college to establish one's qualifications for financial aid. It establishes the baseline cost for college and is used to determine how much financial aid will be awarded by the schools, as well as grants from the government. The FAFSA also must be completed before any student or parent loans from the government can be disbursed.

Profile – The CSS Profile, administered by The College Board, is another financial aid form that is used by about 10% of the colleges in the country—typically the more expensive private institutions. The Profile is a much more complicated application, has over twice as many questions as the FAFSA. It digs much deeper into the family's financial situation than the FAFSA. The Profile also calculates the family's ability to pay for college. Every college requires the FAFSA while some colleges also require the Profile. Some schools require the Profile to be completed each year a student is in college; some require it only the first year.

Expected Family Contribution – Expected Family Contribution, or EFC, is the number (dollar amount) generated by the FAFSA that determines your baseline cost for college. While EFC is not officially a dollar amount, in reality it represents the amount of money a family can afford (according to FAFSA) to pay for college each year.

Cost of Attendance – Cost of Attendance, or COA, is the total amount that a college estimates it will cost to attend college for a full year. COA is the list price of the college and includes tuition, room and board (or cost to live at home or off-campus), books, fees and some miscellaneous expenses like transportation. While EFC sets the baseline for what a family can afford, COA sets the upper limit for what it will cost for that particular college. In general, the wider the gap between COA and EFC, the more financial aid a family will qualify for (assuming your EFC is lower than the Cost of Attendance).

<u>PLUS Loans</u> – Loans provided by the government to either parents or graduate students. Interest rates for PLUS loans are generally much higher than interest rates for other government loans provided directly to undergraduate students.

<u>Pell Grant</u> – A grant provided by the Federal Government. Pell Grants are directly related to a family's EFC and are dispersed only to families with lower incomes. If a family qualifies for a Pell Grant, it will often trigger additional grants and financial aid from the colleges themselves.

<u>Award Letter</u> – The letter sent by colleges that details exactly what the cost will be to the family to attend the university. Award letters are not to be confused with scholarships that may be offered in the initial acceptance letter which is typically sent by the college months before the award letter. Award letters include all grants, scholarships, work-study and loans being offered to the student, as well as to the parents.

<u>Family Economy</u> – This is not a college term, but a term we like to use to describe the financial workings within a family. This includes the family budget, cash flow, investments, debt and income. It is basically how money moves in and out of the family structure.

.

Chapter 1
The College Financial Crisis

In today's fast-paced world, we all have hectic schedules. As parents, you should be commended for taking the time to learn about how the college game is played. We use those words quite deliberately. It is a game—and your outcome is not pre-determined, rather a result of how you played it. Regardless, your investment in this book shows you are genuinely interested in getting your children into the best college available, in the most efficient way possible for your family.

Picture this, as you're standing in the audience on graduation day and as the music starts and the graduates cross the stage, the person next to you says, "Can you believe how much money they gave us to go here? They practically paid us to send our son to this college." And you're thinking, "What are you talking about? All I got are parent PLUS loans that have me saddled with $78,000 in debt I'll be paying off right up to retirement – if I'm lucky!"

The point is this: After your children graduate you can't negotiate. You can't make changes. <u>Your opportunity to get more financial aid occurs before your children start college.</u> This is when you have the most opportunities. You are better off understanding these subtle differences now so you can maximize your award and offers before your children accept enrollment. It doesn't begin with FAFSA in January of your child's senior year; it begins when you start to plan on paying for college – when your children are born. The earlier you start to plan and understand the FAFSA, the more choices and the more control your family will have. This is what we will share throughout this book.

Those who fail to plan, who think they can't benefit from planning, or who assume they can navigate the financial landscape of college, do so at their own peril. Many will unwittingly leave thousands of dollars on the table unnecessarily.

Every family will leave a different amount on the table. We have set up a special website to let you see how much your family will overpay for college and give you a road map to easily reduce the amount of student and parent loans that you will have to take to achieve your child's dream. There is no cost, and this will be the best starting point for most families as they begin the college journey. Go to College Tuition Checkup at www.FAFSACheck.com and start your free college road map.

Brick Walls vs. Speed Bumps

Most families we meet can only focus on what is directly in front of them at any given time. The cost of college is an insurmountable brick wall, an overwhelming mountain that seems like the end of the world. This is especially true if you have more than one child.

Many reading this book are at **Brick Wall Number One: College,** and most people can only see college. **Brick Wall Number Two: Mortgage.** They think once they are done with college they can focus on paying off the house. **Brick Wall Number Three: Retirement.** Finally, they think once they pay off the house they can focus on saving for retirement. By this point, what do you think their retirement looks like? Will they meet their target retirement age or will they be working into their eighties? Will they be able to enjoy the retirement they have dreamed about?

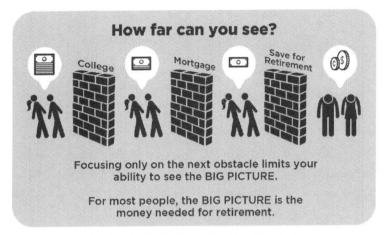

1-1 Brick Walls: How Far Can You See?

Do you know why the parents look disappointed in Figure 1-1? It's college loans—since they spent their whole lives positioning themselves to overpay for college because they did not understand how to leverage FAFSA to their advantage. Everything has been done the wrong way. The parents have amassed a tremendous amount of parent loans and very few for the students. When it comes to college debt, most people think only of student loans. What most don't realize is that parents carry more than 1/3 of the more than $1 trillion of college debt. They have played the game by the wrong rules and have actually been penalized because they were responsible to someone other than their own family. Sallie Mae (bank that services federal-related student loans) and FAFSA take the first position instead of their family. Would you like to see how the rules you have been playing by will affect your retirement from a college standpoint?

Crazy Information

What could you come up with if someone were to ask you, "What is the craziest question you can think of when it comes to the college debt crisis?"

How about this, "How many seniors receiving Social Security are still paying on student loans?"

The answer is both astounding and sad: 706,000—and it is a mixture of both student and parent loans.

Additionally, how many of them are working with that traditional financial planner who told them they should prepare to pay for college well into retirement? How many of them could have saved themselves years of income and hard work by understanding how to leverage the rules to keep their family at the center of the discussion instead of FAFSA, government and the colleges? Most of this debt could have been avoided if they had better information leading up to the college years.

Dig a little deeper and it becomes even more mind boggling. How many American senior citizens are having their Social Security income garnished to pay for student loans? Did you ever think you would hear such a crazy question? Doesn't it sound absurd? Over 155,000 people are actually having their Social Security income garnished (to a reduced amount) just to keep from defaulting on those loans, many of whom had to take Social Security early to pay off their kid's student loans.

They couldn't see the end result once the college process was completed. By focusing on the college brick wall, unintended consequences limited their lifestyle during retirement and created situations that should not happen in America.

The Right Focus During the College Planning Years

It all starts with asking the right question. What is your number one financial goal over the next 30-40 years? For the vast majority of people, it is retirement income. This begs the question, why are we not including retirement as part of the discussion while planning for college? Because the traditional financial world does not understand the consequences of its old ways.

Think of it this way. You are 40 years old when your first child is ready for college. For the next six years (you have two kids, two years apart) you will be paying for college. If you overpay for each kid – $10,000 per year times eight years – that is $80,000 less for your retirement. If money doubles in value about every ten years, then that $80,000 would have grown to $160,000 by the time you were 50, $320,000 by the time you were 60, and $640,000 by the time you were 70. How much different will your retirement lifestyle be with half a million less than you could have had? If you run the math, you will see that you will receive about $40,000 per year less income throughout retirement, all because you were looking at brick walls instead of the big picture.

Compounding this problem, most families don't start planning for college until they get the award letter showing they owe $26,000 for the upcoming school year. Time and time again, we run into families with their first child ready to go to college, who think the student can borrow the full amount needed to attend college. It couldn't be further from the truth. We will shed more light on this later.

If you are able to focus on retirement while you're going through these obstacles, college can become just a speed bump instead of a brick wall (Figure 1-2). Likewise, paying off your mortgage can be a speed bump, and even saving for retirement can be another speed bump because you're keeping the end result in mind.

The best approach focuses on the BIG PICTURE

College → Mortgage → Save for Retirement →

Turn your Brick Walls into Speed Bumps

1-2 Focus on the Big Picture

For families reading this, ask yourself this question again, "What is your number one financial objective for the next 30 years?"

Now that you have had some time to think about it, is it still paying for college? Paying off your home? Paying down debt? Getting your children out of your house? For most people, it's retirement income. The flight attendant tells you to put your mask on first, before helping your child.

The same thing is true with college planning. You must have the best outcome for the two of you. If you focus only on your kids, it will be at the expense of your retirement. Maybe for the first time in a while, you are beginning to think about your goals, instead of following the advice of the financial world, which steers you toward FAFSA, Sallie Mae, and Uncle Sam.

Let's face it, it's your income when you retire, and you deserve all the income you can get. You have spent your entire life working for it. However, while you're going through this college game, it's so exciting, so new, so invigorating, so energetic, it can absorb all your time. You are looking at the brick wall and can't see past it.

Change your perspective so you can see the consequences of paying cash for college over your lifetime. You need to determine the optimum amount to save, a budget to determine the correct amount to pay out-of-pocket for college, a reasonable amount of parent loans, and a working strategy to pay for them. You must do this, all while keeping your number one goal in mind: lifetime retirement income. The results can bring a positive change to your life and, unlike most families, you will not be penalized for being responsible.

Time Is Not on Your Side

Implementing a strategy in advance of the college process allows for much better planning. Before your kids start college, there are myriad things you can do to reduce your costs, but do you know what you can't do? Call a college advisor after your children's graduation and tell her, "I have $180,000 in loans, what do I do?"

She will reply, "Here's your ten-year payment plan, $18,000 a year for ten years. We could have reduced it before your children got through college, but now we can't."

Being proactive on the front end will eliminate the outcome of owing more than you can afford. Even starting a plan three weeks before you file the FAFSA will be better than never starting a plan. Starting a plan years before you file FAFSA opens up possibilities to save money on college that procrastinators will never have a chance to experience.

By now it should be painfully obvious that there is a serious college problem in this country. Gaining an understanding of the problem is an unpleasant, yet necessary affair. Be patient a little longer. Soon, the pieces of the puzzle will start to come together, and by the end of this book you should have a process you can follow that will put you and your family in the driver's seat.

Chapter 2
The Thought Process

KISS – Keep It Simple, Stupid. We all know this often-used acronym. Have you ever thought about just how profound this statement really is?

Traditional thought processes in the financial world will have your head spinning as you chase your tail around and around like a dog. Alpha, beta, theta, derivatives, options, reverse convertibles, triangular moving average—enough complexity to challenge even the savviest investment advisor. We are bombarded on a daily basis with words of wisdom about what to do with our money. Buy this stock. Use only no-load mutual funds. Deal only with ETF's. Buy a 529, UTMA (Universal Transfer to Minors Act) or Coverdell (Education IRA) for college. Buy a pre-paid plan only if your children will be going to a state college.

The problem with all this information is it is complicated. Not that some of these plans won't work, but you need to be an expert to use them properly, and most of us neither have the time nor the desire to become a college or financial expert. We are too busy working and trying to support our families. Worse, when presented with any of these ideas, most people's eyes glaze over.

The true expert will be able to take a plan, complex or not, and reduce it to a simple explanation that can be followed with ease. Furthermore, the best advisors do not use a product at the center of a solution, but instead, they define a custom strategy—a personal road map.

Warren Buffett, one of the most successful investors in history, has two simple rules. Rule #1: Don't ever lose money. Rule #2: Refer to Rule #1. He keeps it simple. Take a step back and you will find that the wealthiest Americans are no different. They keep it simple, but quite different from the average American. Financially successful people will often do things that seem backwards, at least at first. Once they have taken care of the basic necessities like their homes, vehicles, food and education, they begin to invest their extra money in their families and secure their financial future – forever.

Family

After they have taken care of their families and still have extra money, they begin to build a business or buy a controlling interest in one, so they can have something they own and control. They bet on their own strengths.

Business   Family

After they take care of their family and invest in business, they start to buy real estate in order to diversify their portfolio.

Real Estate   Business   Family

After the real estate, business and family buckets are full, they buy stocks, bonds and mutual funds.

Finally, after all of this, they invest in 401(k)/IRA and other retirement accounts – if they have anything left at the end, and if they don't make too much money to participate in these plans.

Did you notice how the previous charts fly in the face of traditional planning? Every time you turn on the TV, you can see another commercial or talking head telling you to roll over your 401(k) into an IRA. Read a book and you will be instructed to pay off your house or "buy term and invest the rest." None of these strategies are found in the previous charts. The last thing wealthy families want to do is invest in something that they can't control, and these strategies are simple.

You should be asking, why do wealthy families work in the opposite direction of the charts above, working from right (focusing on the family) to left (investing in 401(k)/IRA)? It is simple: Working from right to left, they have **more control** over their money, **less risk**, and they **pay less taxes**.

Wealthy people using this thought process, in turn, will typically reduce their EFC (Expected Family Contribution) and what they will pay for college because their approach uses strategies that don't typically count against them on FAFSA. This isn't by design; it is just how FAFSA works.

This also helps explain why average Americans overpay for college and are left with so much student and parent college debt. They are being duped into working in the wrong direction and being hit with the unintended consequence that they will be positioned to assume more college debt. These strategies work well for Americans earning $100,000 to $400,000 per year. When you make $600,000 to $800,000 per year and have one child going to college you won't be able to reduce your numbers enough to get money from the universities. But you may be able to negotiate for a better price. More on that later.

Now let's look at the typical financial planning of the average American worker and how his money works.

He takes as much money as he can and stuffs it into his 401(k). Why do average Americans do that? Because that is what they've been told to do. Over the past several years the government has increased what you can put into your 401(k). It was $9,240 as early as 1995. Then they allowed you to contribute $11,000 in 2002; up again to $15,000 in 2006; and as much as $18,000 in 2015, not including the catch-up provisions for people over the age of 50.

Does the government continue to increase the amount you can contribute to your 401(k) because they recognize that you will need more money to live on when you retire or is it because they need larger pools of money to tax? If the 401(k) was designed strictly for your benefit, then the government would not force you to begin taking withdrawals, and start paying taxes at age 70½.

401 (k)

Perhaps the average American receives a raise at work. His next step might be to start a $200 per month stock account.

401 (k)   **Stock**

Then, he gets a tax refund and buys a duplex with his brother-in-law.

401 (k)   **Stock**   **Duplex**

Next, he buys four gumball machines and puts them in a laundromat.

401 (k)   **Stock**   **Duplex**   **Business**

Finally, if he has anything left over, he secures the future of his family.

401 (k)   **Stock**   **Duplex**   **Business**   **Family**

How is this working out for average Americans? They have less control of their money, they take more risk, and they pay higher taxes. By changing your paradigm, you can level the playing field and play the game the way the wealthy people do. The only difference is perhaps you take a zero off the end of what wealthy people earn and apply it to yourself. This is how you start to plan.

By changing your thought process, you may find that you can reduce your EFC, thereby lowering your overall cost of college. You will also find there are typically two by-products of reducing your EFC.

1. You have more income when you retire.
2. You pay less taxes, like wealthy people.

Even if you can't reduce your EFC for college, there are still positive outcomes for playing within the college rules. Even if you have the ability to pay the list price for college by writing a check, you still need a strategy for paying it off in a way that benefits you more than the FAFSA (government) and the universities.

Paying full price, cash, as you go and not using other people's money can cost you more in the long run, reducing future assets or retirement nest eggs. The reality of the situation is that very few families will actually pay cash for college. Most families will use loans and a budget as part of the process in order to keep the rest of the family economy functioning.

During college you still have to eat, pay a mortgage, pay for health insurance and cell phones, take vacations, buy birthday gifts, and the list goes on. If you pay $20,000 to $50,000 per year for college on an annual basis for several years in a row you won't be able to fund your retirement, take vacations, and your family is out of balance.

Chapter 3
The Economy and Its Impact on Your Ability to Save for College

The most difficult part of the college conversation is talking about money, because no matter where you're at, the subject of money makes for an awkward conversation. As much as people have a love for money, very few ever have an in-depth conversation about it. Most people spend more time planning an annual vacation than they do planning for retirement or college. Before they know it, college is on the horizon. They have no plan, nowhere to turn, and a nauseating feeling of being lost in a dense forest with no clear way of getting out. In order to properly plan for college, you must get serious about money.

One of the first lessons in getting serious about money is understanding how money works from a FAFSA and college perspective. FAFSA and colleges see your money from a much different perspective than you do. The college process has expanded over the past 30 years, but the traditional approach to pay for college has not changed. Getting a modern strategy to pay for college will put you in the driver's seat, instead of trapping you into paying more than your fair share. Following the traditional thought process when saving for college will often result in a situation that will cause you to overpay for college.

Wealth Transfers

It is often difficult to get to the right solution when you start with the wrong premise – saving for college, instead of reducing the cost. As college planning goes, traditionally you really only have a few areas in which you can set money aside. They might involve the stock market; sometimes they involve Education IRA's (Coverdells), or borrowing from a 401(k). There are those who prefer to use real estate. For the ultra-conservative crowd, there is always bank savings.

However, the overwhelming majority of people who are setting money aside for college are using college savings plans, such as 529's, pre-paid plans, MESP's, UGMA's and UTMA's. There are Virginia, Ohio, Indiana plans and many others. The problem with traditional planning is that nearly all of them result in a transfer of your wealth.

What is meant by a wealth transfer?

When we are talking about transfers of your wealth, we are not talking about moving money from your savings account to your checking account. A wealth transfer refers to money moving from your household to someone else's, never to return. Transfers can include market losses, investment fees, credit card interest (especially if you have your paycheck withholding structured in a way that you get a large tax refund each year), and many others.

The largest example of this for parents reading this book is the high cost of college. That $100,000-$400,000 will leave your house and never come back. It is permanently transferred either to the colleges or through loans from Sallie Mae. College savings plans such as 529's, Coverdells and others tend to be market driven, which makes them susceptible to market losses. The cost of college continues to climb at twice the rate of inflation, eroding your ability to save enough while the struggling economy may knock your insufficient savings down even more.

The Way Back Machine...

Perhaps, when you read this, the market is trending upwards and your investments are growing. If not, think back to the last time it was. Think for a moment of the families who, in 2006, 2007 or 2008 had $30,000, $50,000, or $100,000 set aside in 529 plans. After the market crashed they lost five, ten or fifteen thousand dollars from the value of their college savings accounts. The market losses are an example of a transfer of wealth, but not the only one.

Compounding this problem was the fact that many families also had to take out loans to make up for the lost savings, creating another transfer of their wealth through the interest due on those loans.

Someone losing $15,000 in the market who offsets that loss with a $15,000 loan creates a $30,000 swing in their economy, plus interest. Included in most traditional college savings programs are account management fees, maintenance costs and sometimes income taxes (529 plans are usually exempt from capital gains taxes, although there has been discussion in Congress to cancel that benefit).

Even with all these transfers, the overwhelming expense, the largest transfer associated with a traditional college savings vehicle is the increase you will likely pay in tuition. The FAFSA formula, in addition to market risk, will penalize families for having money set aside in one of these programs. Once you reach the FAFSA threshold for what you are allowed to have in savings, you will be penalized at a rate 5.65% of the remaining balance toward your EFC, which will reduce the amount of free financial aid you receive from the colleges.

AHA MOMENT #1

 Did you know that your savings/emergency fund could create a FAFSA penalty?

Think Differently

Think through this for just a moment. A 529 plan works like this:

A family has a daughter who is three years old and a son who is one. In 15 years the daughter will be a freshman in college. They have diligently saved for 15 years within a 529 plan so that when their daughter is a freshman in college, there is an enormous pool of money, highly visible, that the FAFSA and the universities can use to determine how much of their university money they want to set aside to help with the daughter's financial award. They will look right at that large pool of money and say "Mr. and Mrs. College Parent, congratulations for working so hard to save for college! Since you have been so responsible and saved all this money in this 529, we can now use your money first to help your daughter go to college. We can keep our money for someone else! Thank you."

That's the penalty we are talking about. That's the transfer. Now don't think that if you have a 529 plan that you need to rush out and cancel it. Sometimes there is a penalty. Remember there is a threshold you need to exceed before you are penalized. When evaluating whether to keep your 529 plan, you need to look at the FAFSA penalty, market risks, government rules and even whether your children will ultimately attend college.

If you do happen to have a 529 or traditional college savings plan, some exit strategies are smarter than others if you determine that keeping that plan is not in your best interest. Sometimes you will be penalized, sometimes you won't. Penalties vary from state to state, so consult a qualified college advisor. It is important to speak with an advisor who understands not only the 529 rules but also how your 529 impacts your ability to receive money from the universities. Most financial advisors understand the investment rules and penalties of 529 plans; almost none know how much you will be penalized from the colleges for owning one.

Remember that every college is different. Some will penalize you a lot, some will penalize you a little. In some situations, you could see a penalty from community colleges, which provide no free financial aid, because the 529 could erode your ability to get free money from the federal government. Speak with your college advisor.

Some of the more informed families try to avoid 529 penalties by having grandparents own this plan. Grandparent-owned 529's do not need to be listed on the FAFSA. Will these families still be penalized because they were responsible? The answer is yes. It may not directly affect their out-of-pocket cost the first year they file FAFSA, but it can have a tremendous impact the second year of college by reducing the amount of gifting (free money) they receive from the university.

Beginning the second year you file FAFSA, students are supposed to list money received from grandparent-owned 529's. This money is counted by FAFSA as student income and can increase the EFC by as much as 50% of the value of the money pulled out of the 529. Parents can be blindsided by a significant reduction in their financial aid award, and the reduction can be doubled for the third year of college, leaving parents with a situation quickly spiraling out of control. Strategies are available to deal with these issues, but they are dependent on each family's specific situation.

Some examples include waiting until the last undergraduate FAFSA is filed before taking a distribution, using them for graduate school when free financial aid is not so plentiful, or changing ownership on the 529 plan if the state allows it. These strategies and others can be complicated, so consult a qualified college advisor before making the changes. Learning these strategies can help you deal with the situation in a way that puts the family in the best position to maintain control of their college savings.

AHA MOMENT #2

 Traditional college savings plans may increase your cost of college.

The Urgency to Save

As you reach a point in time when your children are getting ready to go to college, there is tremendous pressure on you to figure out how to pay for college. If you have children who are seniors or juniors, you have anywhere from three months to two years before your children go to school. Every financial advisor in the country would tell you that you need to set aside as much money as possible to pay for your children's college, so you don't end up with a student loan problem.

The irony is, every time you turn around, someone or something is stealing your ability to set money aside and save. Furthermore, if you are expected to start saving $1,000 per month now, why have you not been doing it for the past few years? It is unrealistic to think that just because your family is in a time crunch, that money will suddenly appear out of thin air.

While you are getting ready to commit to saving more money, the cost of education is up, the cost of health insurance is up (if we can even determine what the real cost of health insurance is in today's climate). The cost of property taxes is up 50% in the last 20 years. The costs of heat and energy are up. If you go to the gas pump, they make you feel good because you get to fill up for $2.40 a gallon. That feels like a deal when not too long ago it was almost $4.00 a gallon. But it's still expensive.

The cost of water is up, property insurance is up, *everything is going up all around you which is eating away your ability to set money aside and save to help pay for your children's college.* And you are wondering why you don't have huge account balances to pay for college? It is because everyone else has put their hands on your money before you even get to save it.

Let's put this in perspective. A family just had a baby girl. They are expecting their health insurance to increase $200 per month because of the new addition. Perhaps they are ok with that, perhaps not. What really hurts is the additional $500 per month they had to start paying a few months ago because of the new health insurance regulations. This is not a political argument; rather it is a real life example of a transfer. That additional $500 per month or $6,000 per year is eating away at the family's ability to save for college.

Over the course of 18 years, that will amount to at least $108,000 in increased money that will be spent instead of being used to pay for college. With all this going on, it is unrealistic to expect them to save an additional two hundred dollars a month to get their daughter through college. To add salt to the wound, along come taxes, which subtract 20-25% of your income before it even makes its way into your bank account.

For a long period of time, we could say that in the last 12 or 14 years the Federal Income Taxes and Social Security Tax haven't changed that much. Yet, what happened in January of 2013? You looked at your paycheck and they raised the taxes. More importantly, in the last 5-10 years these myriad of taxes have gone up an average of 30%. How many families have had an increase of income of 30% in the last 5 or 10 years? Not many, and those who have are just barely keeping up with tax inflation. We are not able to keep up with the cost of living, regular inflation, devaluation of the dollar, and many other scary scenarios, in addition to the taxes that continue to rise all around us (Figure 3-1).

It is a challenge to deal with all of this pressure and the changing rules. The impact the college years will have on your family can be overwhelming financially as well as emotionally.

3-1 Taxes You Pay

As rules change with colleges, government and the economy, the dynamics within your own family also change. How many families have more than one child? Unless you have twins, multiple children will subject you to more than a four-year college experience. Your college experience could drag on for 8, 10, 12 years or more depending on how many children you have.

Imagine your stress over the first child going to college. Did you pick the right college? Will she be able to get a job after graduation? Will she have a positive college experience? Did the college give you a good financial offer? If you have to spend $200,000 to get your children through college, how does that affect what your retirement looks like or what your life looks like in 10 years?

What does year 11 look like when you have $200,000 less in your 401(k), $200,000 less equity in your home, or $200,000 in additional parent loans? How many years do you have to work to pay that off? How many years do your kids have to live in your house to serve their college debt? How many years do they put off getting married, buying a house, having their own kids—your grandkids, because of the college debt burden?

Now, imagine vacationing on a beautiful island, blue ocean waves crashing to the shore and an umbrella drink in your hand because you get to keep that $200,000 from college. You get to keep it because you took the time to learn how the college game is played. How does that affect your view in 10 years? Feel the stress melt away and how the pressure is lifted. Year 11 has arrived, and you now have $200,000 more in retirement funding, $200,000 more equity in your home or $200,000 less in parent loans! It's a different future isn't it? Now, do you think that what you know today may determine where you will be financially for the rest of your life?

Products or Strategies

Many times in our lives we buy products. Buy a 529, UTMA (Uniform Transfers to Minors Act), UGMA (Uniform Gifts to Minors Act), Coverdell, Ohio plan, Virginia plan, pre-paid plan, etc. Buy, Buy, Buy really means BYE, BYE, BYE to your money. Most families do not even realize they are saying BYE, BYE, BYE to their money for having these plans. The main reason is that most of the information that is out there on the Internet or in the financial world has not kept up with the changing times. It was written 40 years ago and has been regurgitated every year since. What families really need is a strategy, not another product. The goal should be to help you strategize to keep the extra $200,000.

When it comes to college savings, you want to keep your plans in your family's control instead of accidentally creating a plan that benefits someone other than you. We are going to share with you some strategies that keep you at the center of the conversation instead of on the outside looking in. With the right information you will be on the inside making the decisions that are best for your family.

 AHA Moment Recap:

#1 What is your family's limit on savings/emergency funds?

#2 How much should your family contribute to a traditional college fund?

Chapter 4
How Colleges View Your Money

Remember KISS? Let's make this really simple. There are basically three types of money. **Lifestyle money** is the home you live in, the car you drive, the vacations you take or where you go out to eat. **Accumulated money** is your savings, your emergency fund, your money market, your 401(k)s, your IRAs, 529's and other college savings.

Finally, there is **transferred money** which is made up of your tax refunds, your overpayments, your fees and your mortgage expenses. Next to taxes, the most significant transfer you may experience is college tuition. This college tuition could amount to over $100,000 per child that will leave your house forever, never to return, transferred away to Sallie Mae, Uncle Sam and the colleges.

With the three types of money are two types of planning. Traditional planning (old school- created in the 1970's), is borne of the financial advice that was written 40 years ago and has not kept up with the times. Traditional planners use all sorts of complex formulas to determine the perfect amount to save for college. They can account for inflation, increasing tuition rates or rates of return on your savings. However, these plans often require you to make significant changes to your lifestyle.

What is often forgotten is how to account for the true cost of college. Will your children attend community college, a state college or an Ivy League school? Will they stay at home or live on campus? Most importantly, since people rarely pay list price for college, what will be your actual out-of-pocket cost once your Expected Family Contribution is calculated and you receive the award letter from the college listing the discounts they are offering? The one common thread to all this advice is that you are instructed to set large chunks of money aside for college, so you need to save, and save a lot.

Let's look at a true story that is an example of the traditional thought process as it relates to college. To anyone else, this is a funny story, although the lady we are discussing didn't think this was funny. Jennifer had an eighth grader and a third grader and had just gone through a divorce when she met with her financial planner.

If you have met with a traditional financial planner within the last few years, you may be able to relate. You meet with the planner, laying all your personal information on the table. You are then provided a beautifully designed color booklet with a profile of what you need, which says you need $1,200,000 in your retirement account and you need a $1.5 million death benefit if you should pre-decease your spouse. However, the most outrageous part is about college. Here is what this planner said.

"In order to get your children through college and have enough money to pay for it, you need to save $1,200 a month for the younger one and $1,300 a month for the older one." That adds up to $30,000 per year, $2,500 a month pay for college and she only makes $50,000 a year! Can you see a problem with this advice?

Jennifer wondered, "How does he expect me to do this?"

Apparently she is not to buy gifts for her children on their birthdays and Christmas, it must be one or the other. Don't buy another car, don't go on vacations, and don't buy pizza on Friday night anymore. Don't do things that involve lifestyle or savings. There is a great show on TV called "Extreme Couponing." Perhaps she can learn how to do that.

How many people have sat down with someone who has given them this advice and they are serious? They can even say it with a straight face, but that is how traditional planning works. Don't go on vacations, don't fund your retirement and instead, pay for your children's college. In other words, change your lifestyle, now and in the future, to pay for college.

This is one of the biggest problems with traditional planning. Planners think a computer program without any common sense can run numbers and scare you into making decisions to save more money and invest more money, or you will not win. They almost always use the colleges' list price instead of your actual expected out-of-pocket cost to calculate your cost for college, often creating impossible goals to accomplish. They have all the solutions without any of the knowledge. If Jennifer had an extra $2,500 per month, she would not need that person or the computer program.

Modern Planning: A Different Approach

A better type of planning, which is more FAFSA Friendly, would rather have you take money that you are giving away unknowingly and unnecessarily and use those dollars to pay for your children's college education. This way if gas prices rise to $5.00 a gallon your plan is not going to wither away because you will have the extra money to deal with those unexpected surprises.

You are in control, which is a byproduct of reducing your college cost by understanding how to play the game. Since you are making the changes to become FAFSA Friendly, you will have more monthly income while at the same time reducing the cost of tuition. The best way to pay for college is to pay the least amount for the best school, but no one is talking about that. By limiting your transfers, such as tax refunds or overfunding your 401(k), you can free up money for college without changing your lifestyle. More on that later.

AHA MOMENT #3

 If traditional planning transfers money away each month, what is your transferred impact for paying for college?

College debt is soaring faster than almost any other debt. It surpassed credit card debt in 2014 and is second only to mortgage debt unless you count the federal government debt, which had eclipsed a whopping $18 trillion in 2015. Between 1985 and 2015 the Consumer Pricing Index has risen 120% while the average cost of a public four-year college has risen 630%. Students and parents are left with no option except to borrow colossal amounts of money to pay for college, creating a tremendous burden on millions of families.

Do you know the size of your family's college problem? Do you even think you have a college problem? Many families, before they see the light, think they will just figure it out. Many parents think that since they survived college 20 years ago, their children will survive as well. This is part of the traditional thought process. Yet today's college experience is much different from the college experience of 20 or 30 years ago.

In 1982, the average annual cost of college, including tuition, room and board and fees was $3,196. In 2014, the average cost was

$18,943. Your children can no longer work 30 hours a week in the summer to pay for the next year's college cost. The average student today would have to work 52 weeks a year at 30 hours a week to pay for the next year's tuition, and that does not include room and board.

Pay as you go is one option, if it could actually work. It is a viable option, in most cases, to pay for a portion of the costs of college, but you can't expect it to work for the full amount. If you have not already been saving $2,000 per month how can you be expected to start once your kids go to college?

How many families have heard of the $27,000 down payment on college? Do you know about this program? $27,000 is the maximum amount of money your children can have in Federal Direct loans, in their names, over four years of college for an undergraduate degree. So, if four years of college costs $100,000 and your children borrow $27,000, who gets stuck with the other $73,000? You do, the parents. What if the college costs $200,000? If you pay full price and have no savings so far, then you now have a $173,000 problem.

Now, to be fair, it is theoretically possible for students to borrow additional money from private sources, but it is very difficult since most 18-year-olds have no credit history. Parents or relatives can co-sign for a loan, but they become ultimately responsible. Students can sometimes qualify for additional government loans such as Perkins loans, but these are usually reserved for lower income families. While the maximum Perkins loan amount is set at $5,500 per year, they rarely reach that level, usually topping out between $1,000 and $2,000 per year. Not all schools offer Perkins loans.

You can see that it is very difficult for students to be able to finance a significant portion of college through loans, which leaves the parents managing the majority of the financial responsibility.

AHA MOMENT #4

How do you solve a problem without knowing the size of the problem? Are you aware of the size of your college loan problem?

Common Sense and a Little Logic

Should you be concerned about the $27,000 government loan limit for students?

If a student beats the odds and graduates college at age 22 (the national average is about six years), he will have 40 years to pay off that $27,000 loan before retirement kicks in. If your son graduates at 22, how old will you be? How many years do you have until you retire? And if you didn't plan properly you may have $73,000 of expenses or parent loans to absorb.

Compounding the problem is the fact that most families have more than one child. Do the math. Start to multiply this problem by two or three kids. Even if the parents allow each of their children to graduate with $27,000 of loans they could get stuck with over $200,000 in parent loans. The parents do not have the same time frame to pay off this debt. This is equivalent to purchasing a second home and can add a ton of stress to any situation. This is a big problem.

Of course, it is important to control the cost of loans for everyone, including the students. You should weigh many factors before deciding how much money your children should borrow for college. You should consider their earning potential when they graduate, and whether they will continue on to graduate school. Will your children get married to someone with an equal amount of student debt and instantly double their college debt obligation? Without the proper planning, your children could start off their adult lives owing more for college than a nice home. However, in most cases $27,000 is a reasonable amount of debt for someone graduating college, as long as they have the proper plan to pay it off in a reasonable amount of time.

Traditional planning has you overpay for the college experience. Reducing the actual out-of-pocket cost for college through gifting and other strategies can help control the loan problem for both the student and the parents. A 529 college savings plan will not accomplish this for you. Instead of a product, you need a strategy.

Chapter 5

FAFSA: The Foundation
for Financial Aid

How do you apply for aid? If you're going to apply for financial aid, you have to file the FAFSA (Free Application for Federal Student Aid).

In order to receive any financial aid, you must file the FAFSA. Every college in America, from community colleges all the way up to the Ivy's requires it. Whether you want scholarships, grants or student or parent loans, you must file the FAFSA. The only way to get around it is to write a check for the full price of college.

Perhaps you don't want to open up your financial records, personal information and Social Security numbers to the schools and the government. That is your choice, but be prepared to pay full price for college. Before you make that decision, consider a few words of wisdom. The government already has your financial information, and the schools will require your children's Social Security numbers before they allow them to enroll for their classes. The price you could pay for skipping the FAFSA process could make your phantom sense of privacy very expensive.

In addition to the FAFSA, about 10% of the colleges in the United States use the CSS Profile financial aid application. The Profile is administered by the College Board, the same organization that manages the SAT exams. The Profile is used mostly by upper-level private colleges such as Harvard, Notre Dame and others. It is also used by a few public universities such as the University of Michigan. The Profile uses a calculation called the Institutional Methodology, which is similar to FAFSA's Expected Family Contribution. The formulas used to calculate the Institutional Methodology are close, but not exactly the same as FAFSA.

The Profile is not part of the Federal Government, and it is used only by the specific schools that subscribe to it. It assesses your assets differently than the FAFSA does. For example, it will count the equity on your primary residence against you while the FASFA only counts second and additional homes against you. Every $100,000 in equity you have in your primary home will add about $5,000 to your Institutional Methodology number.

The CSS Profile has over 275 questions, many more than the 133 or so from the FAFSA. It asks about what kind of cars you drive, how much jewelry you own, how much you pay for healthcare and many others. It also asks about the equity in the primary home in which you live. There may be additional questions depending on the schools to which the student applies. Harvard is one of the worst offenders, adding 28 supplemental questions to the Profile.

Some schools have their own forms in addition to the FAFSA or Profile. These forms are usually only one or two pages and are not too complicated. If you own a business or a farm, if you are divorced or separated, you may have additional forms. Each school to which the student applies will list their financial aid application requirements on their website, so you should confirm the requirements for each school prior to application.

The FAFSA is a pretty simple form (NOT!). It is only 133 questions and for many years it had 71 pages of instructions. True to government form, in 2015 they added 17 additional pages for a whopping 88 pages of instructions. Perhaps it wasn't clear enough before, or perhaps they needed to publish it before they read it. Go to www.fafsa.gov for the full reference on the rule book.

Once you look at this form and realize most of the questions are ages, birthdates, Social Security numbers, addresses and email, you soon recognize that the 88 pages are for the gray areas like your assets, income and other important pieces of the puzzle. The FAFSA is so complex that it is estimated that 40% of FAFSA applications contain errors. Currently, about 98% of FAFSA applications are filed online, with only 2% sent through the mail.

The electronic version of the FAFSA will catch many errors such as mismatched Social Security numbers and birthdates, unanswered questions and gross misstatements of income. This makes a 40% error rate even more significant. Worse, of the hundreds of FAFSA applications reviewed in our office each year, we discover errors about 80% of the time. In 2015, our team uncovered errors on the FAFSA nearly 100% of the time – mostly to the detriment of the families applying.

While some FAFSA errors will have minimal impact on your ability to receive financial aid, many can have disastrous results. It is highly recommended you have your FAFSA reviewed by a professional college advisor before you file. Once you file, it can be difficult to correct some mistakes assuming you realize that you made one in the first place.

The $18,000 Mistake

So, you're sitting down at the kitchen table, preparing to fill out the FAFSA. You have armed yourself with all your information; tax statements, account statements, your daughter's list of colleges and the 88-page instruction book that you printed at work to save paper. You have a live Internet connection ready to go so you can research questions as they come up.

As you work your way through the FAFSA, you are still not quite clear on how to complete the asset questions, but you are fairly confident you have done enough research that it is accurate enough to file. Besides, you've consumed two and a half hours of your time, half a bottle of wine, four aspirin, and a stress-relief-king-size bar of chocolate and you are tired and ready to get this thing over with. You have setup your Federal Student Aid ID's, checked the button that says you agree to the one and a half pages of terms and conditions and then you click submit. You are finally finished and ready to get a good night's rest.

A few days go by, your FAFSA has been accepted by the Department of Education, and you are on your way, but you have a nagging feeling you should check out that question about your assets. You decide to meet with a college advisor to have your FAFSA reviewed, mainly to put your mind at ease.

While meeting with the advisor, you realize you made a huge mistake. You listed the value of an old 403(b) retirement plan with a value of $320,000 as an asset. After Internet searches and not getting a clear understanding of what counts and where it goes you did what you thought was right. While the FAFSA instructions specifically mention not to include a 401(k), they do not say anything about a 403(b). That's right, even with 88 pages of instructions they managed to leave that one out. What's the difference? It's a mistake that anyone can make, and many do.

The reason you did this was simple. You had changed jobs a few years ago and had started a new retirement account with a 401(k) at the new company. You had converted your old 403(b) into an IRA account with mutual funds invested in the market. Since you weren't contributing to this anymore and it was invested in mutual funds you thought it was a countable asset.

Your heart sinks when you find out that the $320,000 IRA you listed on the FAFSA just increased your Expected Family Contribution by more than $18,000. Depending on the schools to which the student applied, this mistake could cost you anywhere from $4,500 to $18,000 in lost financial aid from the colleges.

Luckily, you caught the error and were able to file a correction on your FAFSA. Just as important, the mistake was caught only a few days after you initially filed, so you didn't lose enough time to make a difference in your ability to qualify for financial aid.

If you think this is a rare mistake, think again. These types of mistakes happen all the time, even to those who read the instructions. The above case is a true story. No names were used to protect the embarrassed.

If you would like a free review of your FASFA, visit College Tuition Checkup at www.FAFSACheck.com to have a certified college FASFA specialist provide you with a complimentary overview.

A Potential Tragedy

Many other problems could have gone wrong with the above scenario. Each college has their own FAFSA Priority Filing Date. In order to qualify for the most financial aid, you must have your

FAFSA submitted by that date. For many schools, the date is March 1, but they can be as early as February 1 or even earlier.

Suppose the filing deadline was March 1, and the mistake wasn't noticed until April 1. Beginning March 1, the financial aid award period begins for students who have filed the FAFSA. Many schools only download the FAFSA application data on a certain day of the week. In addition, it can take up to three days for the FAFSA to be released by the Department of Education, which means that it could take as long as ten days for the college to receive the corrected FAFSA. If the college didn't receive the correction until six weeks after their Priority Filing Date, they may be out of money and you won't receive any additional financial aid.

Another potential problem is that your son or daughter may choose a college that is 2nd, 3rd or further down the list because the financial aid award is not in line with your capabilities to pay for college. If they attend a college that is not their first choice and is not the best-suited school for them, they may spend five or six years completing their degree, costing you even more money.

The worst mistake by far is to not realize that a mistake was made at all. Suppose you would have been due an additional $12,000 in gifting, but all you received was $1,500. You are going to think the whole FAFSA process is a scam, and you may not bother filing again. Compound this problem with two additional students to put through college and you have created a mess that could cost you well over $100,000 in lost financial aid or $100,000 in additional loans, money that can never be recovered. Money that, a few multiples of which, will never be available in retirement or for your heirs.

This is why you need to be very careful to fill out the FAFSA early and correctly. It is also why you should not listen to your neighbors who, even though they make about the same income as you, criticize the financial aid process and claim they didn't get any financial aid. You should also carefully evaluate advice from your financial advisor who may be an expert in growing your money, but hasn't a clue about how to best help you navigate the financial minefield of college planning.

Every family's situation is different, even among equal income levels, so it behooves you to understand the rules and take advantage of every opportunity that comes your way. Preparation is key. Begin the process as early as possible so you can put yourself in the best position to get your child into the best college at the lowest out-of-pocket cost possible.

AHA MOMENT #5

 Each family has a different opportunity that requires a specific strategy.

EFC Revisited: Your EFC and How It Relates to FAFSA

Your EFC, or Expected Family Contribution, sets the baseline out-of-pocket cost to go to any school in this country. The EFC is calculated by a complex series of formulas within the FAFSA. The only way to get your EFC is to file the FAFSA. However, there are many calculators available on the web that can help you "ballpark" your EFC. Some are good; most are not. Many calculators are grossly inaccurate. Many haven't been updated in years, yet the FAFSA formulas are adjusted by the Department of Education annually. If you want your EFC calculated accurately, find someone with a track record for accuracy. Don't trust Internet forms. Find someone you can ask about their accuracy. And beware: *you shouldn't need to pay to have your EFC calculated.*

So what is the EFC and how does it impact your cost for college? If your EFC is $10,000, $15,000, or $20,000, this is what the government says you can afford to pay for college. They won't admit that EFC is a dollar value, but that is exactly what it is (just to make the point, if you look at your student aid report from FAFSA there is no dollar sign next to the EFC).

There are basically two types of gifting from colleges. Merit-based scholarships are based on academics, athletics, music, art and other special talents and abilities, along with how badly the college wants the student to attend their school. Merit-based scholarships have nothing to do with EFC.

The second form of college gifting is classified as needs-based aid. Needs-based aid is derived from your EFC. Your EFC stays the same regardless of which college is under consideration. It doesn't matter whether you go to the in-state public university, out-of-state public university or a private university. Your EFC is the same for all. Schools that use the Profile form will use the number generated by the Profile, called the Institutional Methodology, in conjunction with the EFC.

To keep things simple, we will only discuss EFC, and we will not include merit-based scholarships when explaining how the college financial aid process works, with one exception. Merit-based scholarships will not change from year to year as your financial situation changes. They only require that the student meets the stipulations of the scholarship, whether it is a minimum Grade Point Average or maintaining the talent requirements for sports, arts or other stipulations.

Since your EFC is the same for every school which the student applies, you will pay at least that much for every school that receives your application. The gifting comes into play when the cost of attendance at the school is higher than your EFC. For example, if you have an EFC of $10,000 and the college cost is $25,000, you will have to pay $10,000 but the college could give you up to $15,000 in gifting and loans. What this really means to your family is that you pay your EFC, and if the cost of attendance is less than the EFC, you pay full price. If the cost of attendance is higher than your EFC, you will be eligible for a financial aid award.

When choosing colleges, most families begin by looking at their children's SAT/ACT and GPA to see for which schools they qualify. Geographic location, campus culture, academic programs and school size are all factors that come into play when making a decision.

Of course, the list price for the school is under consideration, as well. Other factors may include how long the average student takes to graduate from the school. Will they get a job, be accepted into medical or law school or have internship opportunities? Is the school faith-based or secular? Is the school on the top 10 list of best party schools? (Most parents can cross this one off the list).

You should generally disregard the list price of the school until you know your EFC. Far more important than the list price is the gifting percentage, and every college has a gifting percentage they meet in regard to the EFC. Going back to the example of the $10,000 EFC, if the school costs $25,000 they may meet 25% or 50% of the difference between the $10,000 and $25,000. If the school meets 50% of the difference, then they will gift you $7,500 and you will pay $17,500.

The reason the list price is not important is that many schools with a cost $60,000 or more may meet up to 95% of the difference. So if a school has a list price of $60,000 and your EFC is $10,000, at 90% gifting they will knock $45,000 off their cost, bringing your actual cost down to $15,000, cheaper than most in-state public colleges. Now you can begin to see some of the opportunities to reduce your cost of college begin to materialize.

A word of caution. Don't get caught up with allowing your children to choose a college based on where their friends go or choosing the top public college in their state because the sticker price is lower than the college they should attend. Marginal selection criteria can be the most expensive way to choose and attend college. Getting started at the wrong college for your child and transferring to another college can add more than $20,000 to your total college cost. Besides, you may find that the higher list-price college has a lower out-of-pocket cost once you receive the award letters.

AHA MOMENT #6

 Every college in the United States has a different cost for each family based on how you fill out the FAFSA. It could be higher or lower than someone with the same income level as you, depending on the FAFSA results.

The lower your EFC, the more money the schools can give you. As the distance between your EFC and the cost of attendance widens, your ability to receive grant money and gifting money increases. By lowering your EFC, you create a larger gap between what you are expected to pay and what the college actually costs, allowing for more gifting from the university. If your EFC exceeds the cost of college, you will pay from your checkbook, or you will make up the difference in loans.

 AHA Moment Recap:

#3 Transferred money will impact your ability to pay for college.

#4 Determine the size of your college problem.

#5 Each family has a different opportunity and requires a specific strategy.

#6 Depending on how they complete the FAFSA, every family has a different cost for college, even at the same income level.

Chapter 6
Leveraging FAFSA to Your Advantage

Why would you want to fill out this offensive form? Unless you want to pay full price, it is a necessary evil. Even if you don't qualify for free money from the university or the government, and you have the ability to write a check for the full price of college, you still might take loans, and for good reason. This could be especially true for your children as there can be some advantages to allowing them to take loans in their names. In some specialized circumstances, the government will forgive a portion of student loans or offer a reduced repayment strategy. For example, if a college graduate gains employment as a teacher, there are programs that allow the student loan balance to be forgiven if it is not paid off within ten years. This same benefit applies to people who choose to work in other public service areas, such as police officers, Federal Government workers or 501(c)(3) non-profit employees. Furthermore, teachers who work in certain economically depressed areas may be able to have up to $17,500 of the student's loan wiped off the book after five years.

Additional programs may be available in the private sector. Some hospitals or medical companies will assist with student loan repayment if a contract is signed upon employment. The same may go for legal firms. It is to your advantage to use someone else's money to help with the college education, if the opportunity comes along.

It almost always goes against your natural instinct to load your children up with any debt. In some circumstances, however, it may benefit you in the long run, as long as you have the right strategy. You need to weigh the options and decide for yourself. Consider the student's expected total debt including graduate or professional school, with or without loan forgiveness, his earning potential and the total interest carry on the loans. You should also consider the impact of not taking student loans on the parents' retirement.

Do not forget to consider how many children will be attending college. If you pay $27,000 extra for three children, that $81,000 could easily cost you $1,000 a month in lost retirement income for the rest of your life. Finally, if you are thinking about taking parent loans instead of student loans, forget about it! Borrowing the $81,000 could cost you an additional $20,000 per year in lost retirement income. If you are looking for loan forgiveness for parents, forget about that too. Parent loans will follow you to the grave.

FAFSA can actually work in your favor by giving you a pathway to avoid sacrificing your retirement to help your children get through college. It allows you to keep your emergency fund, maintain equity in your home, set a budget and control the process moving forward.

Perhaps you have been thinking, "How do the colleges and the government determine if I am eligible for financial aid, especially the free money?"

It is a simple formula: COA – EFC = Financial Need

Financial Need – Gifting = The True Cost of College

Cost of Attendance (COA), minus **Expected Family Contribution (EFC),** equals **Financial Need.** The cost of attendance is the total cost to attend the university, most commonly listed as the annual total.

COA includes tuition, books, room and board, fees and sometimes the colleges will include travel costs. The cost of attendance is set by the individual university.

Remember that the EFC is the amount that FAFSA says you can afford to pay each year. *Your goal is to have the maximum amount of financial need possible* so that you qualify for more of the gifting money offered by the university. Every university will determine the amount of gifting, the free money you receive based on the amount of your financial need. They will award this gifting as a percentage of your financial need and it can range from 0% to 100%.

One of the most misunderstood strategies for FAFSA is how to legally and ethically lower your EFC so that you qualify for the maximum amount of aid available to your family. We refer to this as becoming "FAFSA Friendly." Once your family is FAFSA Friendly, you need to find colleges that are generous and provide higher percentages of gifting instead of just loans.

AHA MOMENT #7

Every family deserves some type of help to pay for college. Some colleges will provide loans and call it a day; others will provide gifting that you do not have to pay back. Your FAFSA and the college to which the student applies determines how much of each you receive.

Traditional Thought Process (Old School)

For the last several years, the general public has received the same college advice on how to pay for college. The problem is, the advice should have changed 20 years ago and every year since. In 1993, the Student Loan Reform Act changed the limits that parents could borrow from the government for college. Until then, loans were capped at $4,000 per year. After that, they were allowed to borrow up to the full amount of the cost of attendance (less any scholarships and other aid). This basically gave a blank check to the colleges to charge whatever they could get away with.

College inflation began, and the cost of college began spinning out of control. The financial world and media (news outlets, Internet articles and financial articles) had learned how to save for college in the 70's and 80's yet never updated their strategy. They have been repeating the same information without adjusting for the changing college world.

Some of the savvier families noticed the high cost of college and got an early start on establishing a college savings plan. Yet the financial world, high on 30-40% rates of return during the 1990's, pushed a thought process in direct conflict with the savings strategies of years before. The traditional thought process had changed ever so slightly, to where you are told to invest rather than save, chasing a greater return instead of preserving your principal. How has that worked out for us in the past 20 years? Our country is experiencing record amounts of debt, people still retire with too little income, and factors outside of your control continue to eat away at your hard earned money.

Think of your grandparents. Do you ever remember them talking about the rate of return they earned from the stock market? Or do you only remember them reflecting that they had been diligent about saving? The older generation doesn't care about chasing a 22% rate of return. They are more interested in preserving the principal. They want to know that they can get to their money when they want it, not have something outside of their control like the crash of 2008 devastate their standard of living. Slow and steady, the tortoise wins the race.

As a country, we have shifted away from preserving our principle to bragging about the 18% we made last year. When the market tanks, all is quiet. Two to three years later when it recovers, the conversations start again. Wait four more years and all is quiet. The cycle repeats itself over and over. How has that shift in thought process worked out for us? By 2014, most people were just getting back to where they were in 2008. Yet they often forget that six years later their money has lost about 20% of the purchasing power it had before, due to inflation.

When your children go to college, you want your hard earned money to be there for you. You need to learn to save in a consistent, dependable fashion with no government strings attached that will penalize you in your ability to receive financial aid. Every dollar that you accumulate needs to be protected, in a way that will not penalize you on the FAFSA.

In one respect, college savings strategies can be similar to retirement strategies. As you get closer to retirement, you should adjust your savings so they are protected against loss, because you will not have time to recover from market downturns. Treat college the same way. Once your kids enter high school, protect your assets so you don't lose money right before they start college.

When planning for college, you must not lose sight of retirement. Your plan for college will directly impact the results you achieve with your retirement plan. The ages of 40-55 and beyond are critical years that will determine your retirement lifestyle. They also happen to intersect the years most of us are paying for our kids' college expenses. Don't sacrifice one for the other. Have a comprehensive plan for both.

The Traditional Thought Process for Retirement Savings

When saving for retirement, the traditional thought process encourages us to overfund our 401(k) to save taxes now. But the reality is that you are likely never going to be in a lower tax bracket than you are today. The thought of retiring to a lower tax bracket at some point in the future probably won't happen.

You may have heard the common advice, "When you retire, you will probably be at 2/3 of your income, and thus you will be in a lower tax bracket." This advice is meant to encourage you to defer taxes now so you will pay less in the future when you spend your assets down in retirement.

Let's look at a family making a decent income of $130,000 per year. Forget for a moment that the country is over $18 trillion dollars in debt, has $96 trillion in unfunded liabilities, and $1.3 trillion in student debt. Assume for a moment that taxes will not go up. In 2015, the 25% tax bracket for a married couple ranged from $74,901 to $151,200. For them to drop to the next lower tax bracket of 15%, they will need to earn 57% of their current income, a far cry from the 2/3 they were promised.

However, this just gains them entry into the next tax bracket. If any real benefit were to be gained, they would need to earn about $64,000, which is 49% of their current income. Do you really want

LEVERAGING FAFSA TO YOUR ADVANTAGE

to plan for a future in which you retire to a lower tax bracket if doing so means cutting your standard of living in half? Do you want to plan for a retirement income less than half what you are currently earning? Does it really make sense to defer taxes to a future date, or would it be better to pay taxes now, especially if they are expected to be higher in the future?

A successful retirement plan for the 21st century needs to stop following the same tired rules that were written in the 1970's. Those who want to maintain their standard of living should strive to maintain, or increase, their pre-retirement income so it can carry them in their retirement years.

Pre-tax contributions to a 401(k) not only impact retirement income, they also have an impact on college financial aid. Every dollar contributed to a 401(k) is counted as an extra dollar of income on the FAFSA. Since these dollars are not taxed, they actually increase your EFC more than if you didn't contribute at all. Each dollar contributed to 401(k) can increase your EFC anywhere from 10-20% of that contribution amount, depending on your tax bracket. In other words, if you contribute $10,000 to a 401(k) your EFC could increase by $1,000 - $2,000.

In most cases, if you receive an employer match on your 401(k) it makes sense to at least contribute up to the match, but anything beyond that would be better directed to a post-tax retirement vehicle. Contributing to a Roth 401(k) does not impact your EFC in a negative way. During the college years, you need to fund your retirement in a way that does not penalize you from a college perspective. It is possible to do both. It is not an either/or scenario, rather an "and" solution that will lead to the best outcome.

AHA MOMENT #8

 According to FAFSA, your ability to fund your retirement also means that you can pay for college.

Who is in Control of Your Money?

The financial world considers the period from 2000 to 2010 the lost decade, from a market return perspective. Two crashes of the stock market eroded savings to the point that most people barely broke even. The Dow Jones and S&P 500 indexes did not even keep up with inflation. There were three dips in the market beginning with the tech bubble in 1999, continuing with the 2001 downturn after 9/11, and climaxing with the disastrous housing bubble that started in 2007. Investment returns averaged less than 3% for the decade.

Nearly everyone lost money; no one was immune, but it wasn't your fault. The loss of your money was a result of external forces and had nothing to do with which mutual fund you chose for your 401(k). Whether it was a terrorist attack, a housing bubble or a financial scandal, it was something outside of your control that created that loss of wealth.

During the mortgage crisis of 2007-2009, millions of people lost their homes to foreclosure. Millions more saw their home equity erode to the point that they were upside down on their mortgages, owing more than what their home was worth. Even several years later, many families nationwide were still trying to recover that lost value from the housing market.

With rising college costs, before the housing bubble, it was a popular idea to use the equity in the home to help pay for college. Hypothetically, it was not a bad plan. Home equity loans were cheap and the interest was tax-deductible. Many families saw their college savings plan eviscerated right before their eyes. Worse, how did that work for those families if their children went to college in 2007, 2008, 2009, 2010 or 2011? The only solution would be to take out expensive college loans at 6 or 7% interest. Just as in the crash of 2001, something outside of their control occurred. Their home values didn't decline because they stopped mowing their lawns, or failed to fix the porch or repair the roof.

Many other factors that can't be controlled impact the ability to save. During the 2007-2011 downturn, wages were stagnant, if you could even keep your job. If you were lucky, you kept up on taxes, which continued to rise. If you were unlucky, you fell behind on taxes, mortgage payments and your credit cards, paying enormous penalties for doing so. Some economists say inflation is right around the corner. Some people say it's already here. The government says we are doing just fine. Yet, the government keeps changing the rules for calculating inflation and economic growth to the point that everything is seen through rose-colored glasses.

It's a funny thing when the government calculates inflation, it excludes things like housing, energy or food. If the government would include these items in the inflation equation, it might be closer to 9-11%. And we wonder why we struggle to save money.

The increasing cost of college has continued to outpace the ability to save. In 2009-2010, the average cost of college rose by 9.5% beyond inflation, and again by 6.5% in 2010-2011. Can you save 6% of your income after you pay for taxes, housing, food, insurance and fund your retirement? The increases since 2014-2015 have shown signs of moderating, but the damage has been done.

Will you be able to retire as planned? Do you know how much money you will need to last your entire lifetime? When you spend $100-$200-$300,000 on college, how does that affect the rest of the picture? Spending more on college will mean you must work longer, have less money for retirement, leave a smaller legacy for your kids and grandkids, have more stress and less control over your destiny. Do you still want to just figure it out? Do you want to remain tied to a traditional financial advisor who is either completely oblivious to the college code, incompetent, or derelict in their responsibility to you or are you ready for a strategy?

AHA MOMENT #9

 You need a strategy to figure out how to pay for college in a way that does not compromise your retirement plans.

More Traditional Thinking on How to Pay for College:

Traditional ways to pay for college, include, but are not limited to:

Buy investments or fund savings only to hope that the college costs don't outpace them. Invest in 529's, Coverdells, UGMA's, UTMA's, pre-paid plans and many others. These are the only traditional ways to save for college. They are more like setting money aside to pay full price for college. Not one of these takes into account the ability to reduce the cost as an alternative to "just saving." You have limited control on these solutions. Market losses, especially right before you need access, can erode any tax advantages of these plans.

Inherit money from your parents or a family member. This would be a great program, if someone didn't have to die first. How does this conversation go? "Mom and dad, you know that I love you, right? However, your granddaughter will be going to college in 15 years. Any chance we can time this inheritance thing?" Perhaps this is not the best conversation to have at Thanksgiving dinner.

Ask for a raise or work overtime. How many people can ask their boss for a raise at work just because they have an extra $20,000 expense for the next few years? Many people may remember growing up when their mom would say, "I'm going to work the double shift on Fridays and Saturdays so we can pay for your soccer or your baseball or your senior ring." Mom could actually get overtime every weekend if she wanted and it was enough to help pay for the extra expenses.

When was the last time you remember being able to work overtime? Today, how many people have the ability to work enough overtime to pay for $20,000 of tuition? You might be able to work enough overtime to make $2,000-$3,000 per year, but not $20,000. Are there enough part-time jobs that pay $20,000 per year? It is not the 1990's anymore, which is why these traditional thought processes do not work. Today's environment requires different solutions.

Borrow from your retirement account. There was a gentleman we worked with who said he was putting as much money as he could in his 401(k) so that when his children go to college he can take that money out and pay for their college. Do you know what the impact is of taking $50,000 out of your retirement account just to pay for your children's college?

It is important to note that 401(k) loans are limited to a maximum of $50,000 or half of your account balance, whichever is less. If you take

$50,000 out of your retirement account to pay for your children's college, you will have to pay it back over five years. While it is true that you are borrowing money from yourself and repaying the loan with your own money, your retirement account suffers during the years you are making loan payments. Instead of funding your retirement with more new money, you're using income to put old dollars back into your 401(k). That could end up costing you $500 a month of your retirement income, from 65 years old until you're 90 years old.

How many people want to take $50,000 out of their retirement pay for their children's college now? And by the way, if you happen to change jobs or get downsized while you have a loan, you will have a whole new set of problems. First, you have 60 days to pay it back or you are taxed (and possibly penalized depending on your age). And while this happens, your income for that calendar year will explode, because that $50,000 401(k) loan is added to your regular income for tax purposes, increasing your EFC, which will cause you to lose more financial aid the next year. You then may have to increase the amount of loans that you have to take, creating a vicious cycle.

Borrowing from a 401(k) for anything is almost never a good idea. When you pay back the loans, those payments are made with after-tax money. So you are paying taxes as the payments go in, then you pay taxes on that money again when you take it out for retirement. You are double-taxed on 401(k) loans.

Choose a lower quality or less expensive school. One of the worse solutions to paying for college is going to the cheapest schools. Many families simply look at the sticker price and do not even apply if it seems out of range. Often, a school with a higher list price actually ends up being cheaper than the bargain school because they offer more gifting.

Often, choosing the lowest cost school does seem like the only solution. Yet how many families have told their children, "If you get good grades, if you do well on your ACT, if you behave and if you're a model citizen, you can go to any college you want?" Perhaps ten years ago when you made that promise, when your children were five, six or seven years old, the cost of college was $10,000-$15,000 a year. Now it's $30,000-$60,000 a year. Can the kids now go to any college they want? No. Now you're saying, "You can go to any college you want, as long as it costs under $20,000 a year." The least favorable criteria on which you wanted to make the best college decision for your child and your family has suddenly become the primary criteria, and no one is happy about it.

AHA MOMENT #10

 Each family will pay a different amount than the published sticker price of the college.

AHA Moment Recap:

#7 Every family qualifies for some type of financial aid. Find out what type your family deserves and which college will give it to you.

#8 Your retirement contributions could actually be hurting your ability to optimize your FAFSA, which takes away potential gifting dollars from the college.

#9 Today's world requires a strategy, not just a savings plan and loans, to pay for college.

#10 It is easier to prepare for college if you know the actual cost you will pay instead of just looking at sticker prices. It also helps to learn which are the best colleges for which your child will qualify and what you will pay. This can open up doors you may have thought were out of reach.

Chapter 7
Follow the Money

Once again, we can look at how traditional planning impacts your ability to pay for college. Traditional planning spends your money differently than you would. The traditional strategies position your family to use your money **first** to pay for college, then they use the government money, and finally they use the university money (Figure 7-1). How many families prefer to be the "first" payer when instead, they can become the last payer?

When colleges evaluate your ability to pay for a college education, they first take a look at how much you can afford, using your EFC as the baseline. Your money is used first. Once they determine how much gifting you deserve, they turn to the government for any assistance, if it is available. Finally, the colleges will kick in their own money to make up the remainder. The colleges use their money last because it puts them in the best position possible.

7-1 Traditional College Funding Strategies

Colleges are a business – a big business! They have a lot of smart people running them, and they know how to win. It makes sense that they use their money last in the cycle of college funding.

However, from a family's point of view, it makes sense that you use your money last instead of first (Figure 7-2). The question is how to achieve this.

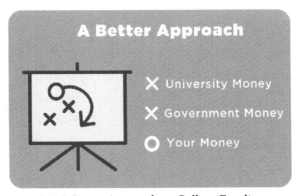

7-2 A Better Approach to College Funding

Saving for college in a way that does not show up on FAFSA will allow you to qualify for the maximum amount of the university's money first. Then it will maximize all available government money. Finally, you'll use your money to make up any difference. It all starts by reducing your EFC before you apply for college and filling out the FAFSA. This simple little strategy will allow you to qualify for more gifted money from the university; and allow you to choose a more generous university, which will help you pay less for college.

The truth is, you've made the best decisions with the information that you've been given up to this point in time. With better information you can make more informed decisions moving forward. The good news is you do not have to change your whole life to take advantage of FAFSA and save money during the college years. Sometimes a small, subtle change now can have a tremendous impact on your final outcome. You simply need to discover the opportunities you have so you can make better-informed decisions.

Sometimes one small change can have a lasting impact on how much debt you carry moving forward while also determining the kinds of colleges that your children attend. With the proper knowledge and strategy at hand, your children can attend the colleges that will provide an experience lasting a lifetime. They will graduate college with a reasonable amount of debt and an opportunity to enjoy a rewarding career. As a bonus, you will be able to retire when you want instead of allowing college debt to dictate your retirement date.

AHA MOMENT #11

 Every family has opportunities, regardless of income, economic status or the type of student you have.

IRS vs. FAFSA

When saving for retirement, the average family follows the IRS tax code to take advantage of any allowable tax breaks so they can maximize the growth in their investment funds. The simplest strategy could start with investing in a 401(k) plan offered by an employer. A person interested in more advanced strategies may consult a professional, perhaps a CPA. CPA's can provide excellent tax-advantaged strategies because they understand the very complex tax codes. A CPA may do this by encouraging you to contribute to your 401(k) to the maximum amount allowed, fund an IRA, max out a SEP (Simplified Employee Pension) or throw as much as you can into a 529 plan. Perhaps you will be encouraged to save interest and increase your tax breaks by refinancing with a 15-year mortgage instead of a 30-year mortgage.

Your CPA may then put you in touch with a traditional financial planner who can help with the decisions and implement the strategy. The financial planner will then tell you to invest in stocks, bonds, and mutual funds, all the while helping you save more taxes by setting you up with the most efficient capital gains strategy and additional tax-deferred programs. Unfortunately, there are several problems that may cause these strategies to work against you.

All of these tax-advantaged strategies may work in the short-term. You may even believe they are working because you see a smaller tax bill each year. However, when you mix college into the equation these plans often do not work. The problem with the IRS tax code is when your children go to college; you get penalized from the FAFSA. For example, the 401(k) contribution will net your family a tax deduction, but every dollar added to a 401(k) increases your EFC, resulting in less free money from the colleges. The same thing happens with a 529 plan, and an UGMA or UTMA, and a Coverdell, and a SEP, and this, and that and many more.

You may receive a small tax savings on a 529. Yet these tax breaks are often wiped out because when the oldest child starts college, the family is penalized on the entire amount of all 529's in the family regardless of who stands to benefit from them. The FAFSA requires you to report all 529's in the family, not just those that will be used for current students.

For example, if you have three children, and each one has $25,000 in a 529, you must report $75,000 of 529 money, increasing your

EFC by as much as $4,238 per year. In much the same way, adding money to a non-qualified account or emergency fund may increase your EFC. Annual dividends or capital gains from stocks will increase your Adjusted Gross Income on your tax return resulting in a higher EFC. While these strategies may work well for a 12-month window, when your kids are in college you may be penalized unnecessarily by receiving less gifting from the colleges.

The Casino Owner

Who always wins at gambling? The casino owner, of course. Just like the casino owner, the government always wins during the college years. The government controls the IRS, FAFSA and the majority of college loans. They win either way, by controlling both sides of the equation. Here are some examples:

When you contribute to your 401(k), you receive a tax deduction for your effort. The money is taken out of your paycheck and funneled into your 401(k) without counting against your income, thus reducing your federal and state income tax. For every $10,000 you contribute to a 401(k) you might save $1,500 - $2,000 in taxes, depending on your tax bracket. However, when you file the FAFSA, you must list your 401(k) contributions, and 100% of those contributions are added back into your income, raising your EFC and reducing your ability to receive financial aid.

Adding $10,000 to your 401(k) could add as much at $2,000 to your EFC. On the surface, it may appear that this is an even exchange, but remember, you eventually have to pay taxes on that 401(k) when you begin withdrawal, and if you are in a higher tax bracket when you retire this only compounds the problem. Worse, lost financial aid is money you will never recover again.

If you manage to save $20,000 into an UGMA or UTMA, you will receive a small tax break because the earnings are taxed at the children's tax rate. UGMA's, UTMA's and any account that has the children as the primary account holder is slapped with a hefty 20% penalty on the FAFSA, so this $20,000 UGMA will increase your EFC by a whopping $4,000. Note that regardless of whether the owner is a parent or the child, 529's are not considered a child asset so they incur a smaller penalty, about one-fourth the penalty of a child asset.

Sallie Mae is the largest servicer of student loans in the country, controlling over 20% of all student loans. While Sallie Mae changed from a government agency to a private lender in 2004, the U.S. government continues to be heavily entwined in Sallie Mae (much like the U.S. Postal Service). The government expects to earn more than $135 billion from Sallie Mae over the next decade. Whether you pay more taxes or take out more loans for college, the government wins. The important thing to do is to reduce your cost of college and reduce the amount of loans you take out.

AHA MOMENT #12

 Your IRS strategy may increase your EFC, which could create more PARENT loans and a higher cost of college!

While your children are in their college years you have to play by different rules. Instead of focusing on the IRS tax code, you need to focus on the FAFSA college code. During the four, six or eight years that college is in your plans, you need to change the thought process to protect what you have worked for and keep your hard-earned money in your family economy, instead of giving more of it to the FAFSA and the government. Then, when your children get out of school you can go back to doing things the way that you've done them before.

What is Your Plan to Pay for College?

Typical plans to pay for college may include Roth IRA's, 401(k)'s, college savings, student and parent loans or simply writing a check. Yet, the most expensive way to go to college is not to have a plan at all. Don't fall into the trap that you will be able to figure it out once your child gets accepted to college and you receive the financial aid award. By then it is too late, and it will cause you to overpay massively for college.

Here is an example of a family's approach to paying for college.

Sitting around the dinner table, the subject of college is brought up and quickly leads into a discussion about how to pay for it. Since they haven't saved any money yet, both parents look at each other waiting for the other one to say something. Since there is no money, no plan and no understanding of how the college game is played, there is dead silence. Sometimes it may turn into an argument. If a strategy is mentioned, it can feel like throwing darts at a dart board, hoping to hit the right number but with your eyes closed.

With no real factual information, the solution does not exist. After a short time, the conversation turns to something else and it doesn't get brought up again for a long time. As college nears, a last ditch effort is made, only to finally decide that the kids will have to pay for it with student loans. When the award letters arrive, the parents are in shock when they see a bill for $25,000 for the upcoming year, only $5,500 offered to the student in loans and $19,500 offered to the parents in parent loans.

The above scenario may seem far-fetched, but it is much more common than you think. Having no plan is by far the most expensive way to pay for college.

The Perfect Tuition Payer

Who is the perfect tuition payer? Becoming the perfect tuition payer is not a good thing. The perfect tuition payer will overpay for college, and is a title you do not want on a plaque on your wall. If two or three of the following scenarios fit, then you may be positioning yourself to significantly overpay for college.

You trust a professional to give you advice.

There is nothing wrong with seeking out professional help. In fact, it is highly encouraged. However, make sure the person you are dealing with is up to date with current college strategies, and not using a traditional thought process to plan for college. Beware of the person who suggests funding a 529 or paying down your house so you can use the equity in your home to pay for college.

Your children are excellent students who test well on the ACT or SAT and are involved in high school activities.

Again, there is nothing wrong here. Everyone wants to have children who excel at school, and all children should be encouraged to do as well in school as possible. Problems can arise when schools are selected that don't fit well with the student's academic ability, leading to transfers to other colleges mid-stream, lost credits and a lengthened time before graduation.

The parents have a budget for college but it doesn't include upscale universities.

Don't get caught in the trap of choosing a college based only on the sticker price.

The family has more than modest means, which by FAFSA standards means an income greater than $80,000 per year.

The EFC begins to increase very rapidly once the income reaches $70,000 - $80,000, depending on the number of people in the household, so proper measures must be taken to control the EFC. Choosing schools that offer higher levels of gifting becomes more important once the parents' income reaches this level.

The family has established a financial plan, sometimes with a professional financial planner.

Beware of using a financial planner who is not up to speed with the latest college strategies.

The family contributes to college funds.

Saving for college is a necessity, but care should be taken to save in a way that won't penalize your ability to receive financial aid.

One or both of the parents is a business owner.

Business owners have additional opportunities, especially to reduce the adjusted gross income. Ensure that you take advantage of these opportunities.

If two or more of these scenarios apply to your family, you are at risk of overpaying for college.

AHA Moment Recap:

#11 Every family and every student at every income level has opportunities to reduce the cost of college.

#12 Planning your financial strategy around your tax refund creates IRS vs FAFSA stress, potentially increasing your cost of college.

Myth and Reality

Myth after myth surround the FAFSA. FAFSA is such a complicated process it is no wonder there is so much misinformation weaving its way through college families. If you review hundreds of FAFSA's a year as we do, on the surface FAFSA can quickly appear to be a fairly simple process. Yet since every family has a unique situation, underneath the "simplicity" of the form lies a complex system of interpreting the rules that are not always black and white.

One common myth that rears its ugly head is, "My income is too high. I'm not going to file the FAFSA because I will not receive any financial aid anyway. I will just hope for scholarships and pay the remainder with my checkbook."

While it is true that many families who have done well for themselves will have an EFC that is too high to qualify for needs-based assistance, even they may create opportunities for themselves by filing FAFSA. Sometimes they may have an opportunity to negotiate a lower tuition by introducing a competing college into the mix and FAFSA is the starting point.

Even more problematic are families who would actually qualify for needs-based assistance by filing FAFSA, but choose not to do so because of someone else's situation. Take a look at a not-so-uncommon situation:

Your neighbors down the street have a child who is a year older than yours. You know they probably make about $5,000 less than you because you are good friends, and you also heard their complaints when they filed FAFSA and didn't receive any money from the in-state public university.

So you think, "That family didn't get any money. They make less than I do, so I'm not going to bother to file it. I'm not filling it out."

That could be a costly mistake. Many families around the country follow this same myth, yet they don't understand that every family situation is unique. What if your neighbor has a countable asset worth $150,000 that you don't have? That could mean an extra $8,500 added to their FAFSA. What if they only have one child and you have three? Those extra two children, even if they are not in college, could reduce your EFC by $4,700.

Finally, what if they made a mistake? This is the saddest scenario. Not only would they stop filing FAFSA because they didn't get any financial aid, but they have convinced another family to lose out on potentially thousands of dollars in free money, all because of one mistake on a FAFSA.

Don't allow yourself to get caught up in the misinformation. Of course, you should be planning on helping your children with college, but as you save, you should be setting the stage to be FAFSA Friendly so that when your oldest is ready for college your assets are protected and you will qualify for the gifting money.

More importantly, you should make sure your FAFSA is completed accurately every year so you don't blow an opportunity to reduce your cost of college. Remember, the earlier you start the process, the better because you have more ways to save that can put your hard earned dollars to work for you as efficiently as possible.

Stan's Big Mouth!

When Stan Targosz was in his younger days, before he was so refined, calm, cool, and collected, he was talking to an audience of 120 families and he said, "I can help anybody regardless of your income."

After the event, a gentleman came up and said, "Were you serious about that income comment or were you just trying to impress us?"

And Stan said, "Yes, of course I am serious about the income."

The parent said, "Good. I'm a doctor, making about $400,000 a year, and I have one kid left to go to college."

Stan did his best to keep his composure, but deep down he was thinking he opened his mouth just a bit too soon. This was early on, when we were just entering the college planning business, so Stan just didn't know what he didn't know.

The Rest of the Story

Interestingly enough, the story ended up with a happy ending. Even with advanced techniques to try to reduce the EFC, in this case the doctor's Adjusted Gross Income (AGI) was still too high to be able to reduce his Expected Family Contribution to receive needs-based gifting from the college his son wanted to attend.

While reviewing his finances, it was discovered that he was helping his mother by paying several thousand dollars per month that was not credited on his tax forms. This allowed us to write an extreme circumstance letter to the colleges and some of them responded by reducing their price. This is not the end of the story. It gets better.

The son was encouraged to apply to a few more schools he did not have on his radar for the purpose of negotiating with the college to which he wanted to go. When he received the financial awards, he submitted them to the top three schools. When all was said and done, he received an additional $16,000 per year off the cost of his top choice college.

Does this happen for every family? No, but for him, it worked. You do not know what opportunities you may have until you put a strategy in place and ask with specific intent.

AHA MOMENT #13

Many families have some control over how much money they get from the universities. You can increase the amount of money you get based on how you position yourself and what strategy you put in place.

Myth

There are many families who live in very nice homes, as much as $500,000 or more. They think that the colleges won't give them a dime. Interestingly, the actual value of your home doesn't factor into the financial aid formulas. Instead of your home's value, colleges look at the amount of equity you have available. Their goal is to find how much money you have available to pay for college.

Colleges will typically count everything they can, with the exception of assets that you would be penalized to access; hence the reason 401(k) balances don't count against you. Since you can access the equity in your home without penalty, colleges see that as a potential option to pay for tuition. Therefore, even if your home is worth $800,000, if you have no equity in your home then it won't count against you.

What if your home is paid off? You may be worried that this will crush your ability to receive financial aid. The fact is not every school counts your house against you, even if it is paid off. FAFSA will not count the primary home that you live in against you. This means that all schools who use only the FAFSA for financial aid determination will not count the home you live in.

About 90% of the colleges in the country use only the FAFSA. The remaining 10% use the Institutional Methodology as provided by the Profile application administered by the College Board. These Profile schools do count your primary home's equity against you. All schools will count 2nd and additional homes against you. If you have a significant amount of equity in your home, don't rush out and take a loan against your home because you think you will be penalized.

There are many options to prevent your home equity from counting against you, but you need to have a professional assess your situation to determine your best strategy. The strategy you choose for dealing with a home depends on many factors, such as the cost of attendance at the schools you are considering, your EFC with the house out of the picture and the gifting generosity of the schools on your list. Considering the amount of equity in your home(s) can be an important part of your college strategy and can help you in your quest to protect the family resources, especially if you are looking at a Profile school instead of a "FAFSA only" college.

AHA MOMENT #14

 You might pay extra money for tuition if you have been responsible and made extra payments to reduce your mortgage and increase the amount of equity that you have in your home, especially if your kids go to a college that will penalize you for having home equity.

Myth

Many people believe their child doesn't qualify for needs-based aid so there is no hope.

The fact is, even if your EFC is too high for you to qualify for need-based aid, there are many ways to obtain financial aid that is not based on your ability to pay for college. You may still receive scholarships, grants and money received through negotiation. Many private colleges, especially the colleges in the middle of the pricing range, will award money simply because they want to compete on a pricing level more in line with the cost of public universities.

This is not too much different than paying 30% less for an item at your local home goods store. The tag may have a manufacturer's suggested retail price of $50, but the store has it listed for purchase for $35. Private colleges must maintain a perceived value that you will get a better product from them than the public university, and in most cases you will, but they must also remain competitive with their actual cost or no one will be able to afford to attend.

The government also has an influence on the higher cost of private colleges. Unlike public colleges which receive millions of dollars of state funding, private colleges do not receive state funding. This lack of funding forces them to charge more for their cost of attendance. You see the same impact of government subsidies for public colleges by looking at how much public colleges charge for out of state students. Have you ever noticed how the out of state tuition for public colleges is as high as many private colleges? The cost of attendance for the University of Virginia for the 2016-2017 school year is $30,500 for in-state residents and $59,800 for out of state non-residents. Attending an out of state public college can often be the most expensive way to attend college, because their gifting percentages are often much lower for non-residents than they are for residents.

In addition to the list price discount, there are several million dollars a year that go unclaimed in the scholarship arena. How much of this you can receive depends mainly on how much effort the students want to put forth to find scholarships for which they can apply. While scholarship money can certainly help with lowering the cost of college, it should not be the main focal point of your strategy, because scholarships are very subjective. Furthermore, many are not renewable from year to year so your costs may increase after the 1st year of college. Find schools that are more generous with their money first, then add scholarships if you can.

Myth

It's a simple, easy and fair process.

FAFSA is not the **FAIR** Application for Federal Student Aid. It's the Free Application for Federal Student Aid. College financial aid, with the exception of Federal Pell Grants and loans, is mostly unregulated. As you will find when we cover two case studies later in this book, there is little about the FAFSA that is FAIR. The government sets unrealistic expectations about how much you can afford. It often appears as if they want to make you assume large amounts of debt and OWE the GOVERNMENT more of your money to get your kids career-ready. Paying for college is a crazy game, and if you are unaware of the consequences, you will overpay and have larger student and parent loans.

College is expensive no matter where your children go, because it's not just about the tuition. You have to pay for books, room and board, living expenses, pizza money, football tickets, travel to and from, health care, phone bills, technology fees, sororities, fraternities, visits home for holidays and so much more.

Four years can cost from $80,000 to $200,000 or more. Multiply this out by the number of children in the family and it quickly gets very expensive! And costs continue to rise every year. Finding a way to pay for college will most likely be a very stressful chapter of your life. Your payments could stretch out for 10 years or more, even with one child. Many people don't consider this when formulating their strategy.

How many families would buy a vacation home for $250,000 and pay for it with a four or eight-year mortgage? You wouldn't because it would tragically affect your ability to live, fund your retirement, build your emergency fund, pay off your primary residence and enjoy life. Yet many families think they will pay for college in the same time frame, while not realizing that it will cost as much as that vacation home. Whatever strategy you put in place must help you pay for college in a way that keeps you in control.

AHA MOMENT #15

Having a budget and a plan that keeps you in control might mean changing your priorities during the college years. Your mortgage, traditional retirement contributions and college savings plans are just a few of the approaches to your finances that need to be reviewed and realigned.

The Rising Cost of College

The average annual cost of a private university is about $45,000. The average cost of a public university is about $22,000 and costs have historically risen at two to three times the rate of inflation. Between 1984 and 2014, college costs skyrocketed by 146% for private four-year colleges and a whopping 225% for public four-year colleges.

The cost of college is rising so quickly that families cannot keep up. How many families, when they went to college several years ago, thought they would ever see a college cost $60,000 a year? In 2015, some schools surpassed the $70,000 per year cost (Figure 7-3). How soon will it be before we see $100,000 per year?

ACTUAL COLLEGE COSTS

Including tuition, fees, room and board only.

School	Cost	
	Current	5 Years Ago
University of Michigan	$ 27,812	$ 24,131
UCLA	33,898	25,497
Yale	65,725	49,800
Northwestern	68,060	52,463
Penn State	35,532	29,684
Arizona State	25,940	21,924
NYU	70,444	40,082

7-3: Actual College Costs

The high cost of college does not appear to be a deterrent for people to apply. Admissions are up. The government is no help since they continue to allow every family to borrow the full amount of the educational experience. Unlimited funding means there is no consequence for the colleges to increase their tuition, yet payment for the education is financed through loans on the backs of the parents.

A common approach to keeping the cost of college at a reasonable level is to send your kids to a public in-state college. After looking at $50,000 to $70,000 a year colleges, $20,000 a year may seem like a good bargain, yet don't forget to consider the incidentals. If you add wardrobes, transportation, insurance, medical, personal expenses and pizza money, the first year's total could be $25,000. If you factor it out with inflation over four years, the total cost could be $109,000. That is substantially higher than the original $80,000 you started with.

Eventually, your kids graduate and they move back home for a couple of years, decide to get married, and you get to help pay for their wedding and then finally help them move out of the house. My mom didn't think that was funny either.

Factors That Influence Your EFC

What impacts a family's ability to receive financial aid? As you have already seen, your Expected Family Contribution plays an important role in your ability to receive financial aid. When you complete the FAFSA, complex formulas are used to calculate your EFC. The government uses this EFC to determine how much you can afford to pay for college each year, and the colleges use the EFC to determine how much gifting you will receive. Once you have a basic understanding of what factors impact your EFC, you will be on the road to becoming more FAFSA Friendly.

The Age of the Parents.

As a parent, whether you are 40, 50 or 60 years old determines how much money you are allowed to have in the bank before the FAFSA penalizes you. This is based on the oldest parent in the relationship. In a single parent situation, FAFSA uses the age of the parent who is listed on the FAFSA application. Age is one thing you can't control, but being older has its advantages according to FAFSA. If you are 50 years old, you're allowed to have about $35,000 in countable assets before you receive a penalty. If you have more money in your household than you are allowed, you should assess exactly how much those assets count against you and decide on the best strategy to deal with it.

The Size of the Family

The number of members in your family has a significant impact on your EFC. The larger your family, the lower your EFC. The difference between two members in your family or seven members could make as much as a $9,400 difference in your EFC. While you don't have much control over the size of your household, you do have control over reporting it accurately. The number of dependents you list on your tax return has no impact on the number you list in your household on the FAFSA. While it is true that FAFSA does ask how many dependents are listed on your tax return, this question is used only as a check for accuracy in completing the FAFSA and does not impact your EFC.

The correct way to list the number in your household is to count every person who lives in the house and for whom the parents provide more than 50% financial support. Therefore, if you have a relative living in your household and you provide the majority of his support, you can count him as an extra member of the household and lower your EFC.

Adjusted Gross Income

Your income has by far the largest impact on your EFC than any other factor. If you can lower your AGI (Adjusted Gross Income), you can reduce your EFC. Depending on how you receive your income, there may be opportunities to reduce your EFC significantly. If you receive income through a 1099, you may be an independent contractor and may have many tax deductions that can reduce your AGI. If you are a business owner, you may have more opportunities, even if you earn a high income.

In these situations, it can work in your favor to have a skilled tax professional in your court. Keep in mind that most tax professionals do not understand the impact their changes will have on your FAFSA, so you need to have a qualified tax person and a college professional working together for your benefit. If you are a W-2 employee, your options are more limited than others, but you still have opportunities depending on your situation, especially regarding your retirement contributions.

Retirement Contributions

Many people have heard that retirement has no impact on your ability to get money from the universities. The truth is, the value of your retirement doesn't harm you but your annual contributions do. Contributions to a 401(k), traditional IRA, SEP or other similar tax-deferred account will increase your EFC. Contributions to these types of accounts are added to your FAFSA and count as additional income.

While you don't want to stop funding your retirement while your children attend college, you want to fund it in a way that doesn't penalize you and increase your EFC. There are ways to fund your retirement, not get penalized on the FAFSA and keep your family at the center of the solution instead of the government.

Home Equity

Several years after the 2007 housing bubble burst, many families finally began to realize some equity in their homes. After 2007, families became very conservative with their spending and more protective of their savings for fear they may experience another crisis.

Many people began accelerating their payments on their homes so that if a crisis does occur, at least they will not have to worry about losing their home.

Since extra payments on a mortgage increase the equity in your home, and may increase your EFC, you may be better served by saving that extra money in a way that won't penalize you for college. If you don't end up using those extra savings to pay for college, then you can simply pay down your mortgage once your kids have graduated.

In a low-interest environment, a $100,000 mortgage may cost about $442 per month, tax-deductible. If you have to take loans, would you rather pay $640 per month at 6.4-7.9% for a student loan, non-tax deductible, or $442 per month tax deductible? Choosing the $442 a month as a loan against your home could also lower your EFC if your children are attending schools that penalize you for equity in your home.

You may consider changing your approach to your finances, at least while your children are going to college. This goes back to the IRS code vs. the FAFSA code. For the college years, you have to play by different rules. Don't fall into the trap of using traditional advice instead of what is required in today's environment.

Non-Qualified Accounts

Non-qualified accounts are savings that do not qualify for a tax deduction. Under most tax law, a non-qualified account can be thought of as any account that is not penalized if you access the funds before age 59½. Non-qualified money includes money market funds, mutual funds, stocks, bonds, bank CD's and your emergency fund.

The amount of non-qualified money that you have has a direct impact on your ability to get financial aid. Once you're above your FAFSA savings threshold, you are assessed a penalty on every dollar you have in non-qualified accounts. Each family is different. The threshold for a family when the oldest parent is 44 years old is $30,000. However, in a single parent household, if the parent is 44 years old, the threshold is only $6,900. Apparently, a single parent family needs less savings than a dual-parent family. Remember, it's not the "FAIR" Application for Federal Student Aid.

AHA MOMENT #16

 It is a great idea to maintain an emergency fund, but structuring it the wrong way may cause you to overpay for college.

Children's Income and Assets

Penalize responsible children, too? Say it ain't so!

How many people have children and they want them to work? Come on now, everyone should be thinking, "Me."

This is a no brainer. You may be thinking, "Wait a minute, what's that I see, another penalty?"

Do you want your children to save the money or spend the money they earn? Save it, of course. Yet once again, when someone is responsible, the penalties come rolling in. Once the student surpasses the income threshold, there is a 50% penalty added to all additional income. Fortunately, most children don't surpass this threshold, because it can be as high as $7,000 per year depending on how many taxes are paid.

Don't let out that sigh of relief just yet, though. If your child is resourceful enough to save her income, she will get penalized on those savings at 20%. To add salt to the wound, there is no threshold on savings for dependent students, so as soon as the savings surpass $5.00 the penalties begin to accrue. If a student's earnings surpass the income threshold, and that money is deposited in the bank, she could be penalized a whopping 70% of every dollar. This quickly becomes a way to increase your EFC and lower potential gifting. For every $1,000 earned above the income threshold and put into savings, $745 could be taxed or added to the EFC.

How Quickly Can Your Problem Grow?

Every dollar you have in savings, income and home equity can quickly ratchet up your EFC, eroding your ability to pay for college. While Figure 7-4 serves as a useful example of just how fast your EFC can spin out of control, it is also a perfect example of how much opportunity you may have, given the right strategy.

Impact on EFC*
FAFSA and CCS Profile Savings

Asset	Asset Value	Calculated EFC*
Adjusted Gross Income	$ 100,000	$ 20,000
Equity in House	100,000	5,640
Emergency Funds	100,000	5,640
529 Plan	50,000	2,820
401 (k) over match	12,000	1,800
Student's Savings	10,000	2,000
Total Expected Family Contribution		$37,900

Making the assets "EFC Friendly" Reduces total EFC to $20,000
*EFC = Expected Family Contribution.

7-4 Asset Impact on EFC

Assume for a moment that you have an Adjusted Gross Income of $100,000 per year. Your starting point at this income level may be around $20,000 for your EFC. Of course, the EFC at this income level can vary widely depending on family size, tax liability and other factors, but $20,000 is a reasonable starting point for this example.

Every $100,000 of equity in a home that counts on FAFSA or the Profile form will add $5,640 to your EFC. The same goes for emergency funds and 529 savings. Overfunding a 401(k) by $12,000 could add $1,800 to your EFC. A sizeable savings account owned by the student could add $2,000.

In this example, using traditional savings strategies has increased the EFC from $20,000 to $37,900, which could result in almost $18,000 per year in lost financial aid for some schools. This could be a $72,000 mistake over a four-year period, and that is for one child who graduates in four years. Multiply this by two or three children and you have just cost yourself $200,000 or more in lost financial aid that could have been used to fund your retirement.

In an average market this mistake could cost a family $35,000 or more per year in lost retirement income. This would be a tremendous mistake for sure, but positioning yourself correctly before the college years could make or break the chance to have a comfortable lifestyle during retirement. Therein lies the opportunity.

Stan's Jet Ski

When Stan was a kid, he attended a private school. They had this great program starting in February where they sold raffle tickets and then they earned "free" days, days when they did not have to go to school. It was the best incentive program ever. Stan had every Friday off from February to June.

Stan's dad owned a manufacturing shop and he said "Listen, you're not going to at sit home and watch TV. You're coming to the shop and you're going work."

So he worked every Friday and Saturday and in the summertime he worked overtime. Within a year, he made over $12,000. His dad was very proud because he made him save $5,000 of his earnings. Back then, the income limit for students was about $2,000, so $0.50 of every dollar he made above $2,000 was added to the EFC calculation. He made $10,000 more than his limit. **His family had a $5,000 penalty,** which reduced how much money he received from the university.

Stan's dad could have deferred his compensation or implemented another strategy. He could have done ten or fifteen other things.

Then, the $5,000 he had in his bank account that he saved, caused him to lose another $1,000.

Every time Stan sees his dad, he reminds him, "I would have been better off buying that jet ski that I wanted instead of being smart and responsible." Stan's dad still doesn't agree.

1970's College Planning

College planning in the 70's suggested having your kids four years apart so you would not have to pay for college two times in any given year. This strategy may have worked then, but times are quite different now. Beginning in the 1970's and continuing through the 1990's the length of time required to complete a college degree increased significantly. The number of college credits required to complete a degree slowly increased from 120 credit hours in 1970 to as high as 138 credit hours in 1990. State legislation in the 1990's began limiting the maximum amount of credits to 120 credits again, yet even with new legislation the average time to complete a degree is 5.7 years today.

It is not reasonable anymore to consider having your children six years apart to avoid paying for more than one college degree at a time. In addition, even if families decided to wait to have children, each year they wait, the cost of college tuition continues to increase faster than the rate of inflation, so how can anyone possibly keep up? Fortunately, there is hope.

The Multi-Child Discount

Remember that the EFC determines your baseline cost of college. Your Expected Family Contribution is the amount you pay for college no matter where your children go to school. If your EFC is $20,000 and you have two children in school, it is $20,000 for student A and $20,000 for student B, right? No! It is $10,000 for student A and $10,000 for student B, even if they go to different schools.

The EFC is a family contribution, not a per child contribution. If you have more than one child and they are close in age, when both are in college, the gap will be wider between your EFC and the cost of attendance at their colleges and you will receive a discount.

Now it is vitally important to determine the financial aid that is given by the university that the older one attends because when the younger one is in college, you could be positioning yourself to get a significant discount. This is a tremendous opportunity and is one of the most under-utilized strategies for families. Do not forget to factor in the multi-child discount when planning your college future.

Also, confirm with the financial aid officers at the colleges under consideration that they will increase the award for the first child when the second child enters college. Most colleges will provide a discount if it is justified by the lower EFC, but sometimes they need a little push when the second child enrolls. You should confirm the increased award before selecting the college, and you may need to contact the financial aid office to remind them they need to make an adjustment when the award letter is issued during the lower EFC years.

There is one caveat. Colleges that use the Profile form in addition to the FAFSA will not generally provide a multi-child discount if the sibling is attending college part-time or is attending a community college. The Profile form asks for the schools each student in the family is attending as well as how much the family will be paying for those students.

AHA MOMENT #17

 Every college provides different levels of free money, making the sticker price secondary.

AHA Moment Recap:

#13 A lot of families have an opportunity to increase their financial aid award by putting themselves in the best possible position financially.

#14 The equity in your home may be creating a higher college payment than the mortgage payment.

#15 Being responsible during the college years requires a different budget strategy. Determine the most efficient path to saving money on college.

#16 Your family is only allowed so much in an emergency fund. Every family is different. Make sure you are not in the penalty zone.

#17 Every college will gift at a different level. Check to see if the colleges you are looking at have a track record of being generous.

Chapter 8
Case Study #1: Steve

It is time to walk through a case study. Two case studies will be covered. They have been chosen in order to provide an overview of two completely different financial and family situations. They are designed to exhibit opportunities that are available to families to reduce their out-of-pocket cost for college. Both case studies are based on actual family scenarios. The names have been changed to protect the innocent and all that fun stuff.

Let's dig in. Steve is a 55-year-old business owner. He's married with two children, ages 15 and 17. Steve makes $250,000 a year, has a mortgage of $150,000 and a home that is worth $350,000 (Figure 8-1). He is paying $1,800 a month for his mortgage as well as $400 a month extra so he can accelerate the payoff of the loan.

Steve has retirement savings of $400,000. Since he is a business owner, he generally doesn't receive a tax refund. At the end of the year he owes money. He has debts of $30,000 for which he is paying $1,500 a month. These payments are not out of range for a person of his income and lifestyle.

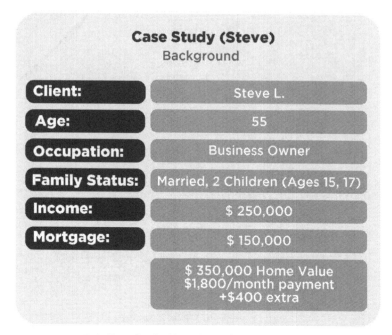

Case Study (Steve)
Background

Client:	Steve L.
Age:	55
Occupation:	Business Owner
Family Status:	Married, 2 Children (Ages 15, 17)
Income:	$ 250,000
Mortgage:	$ 150,000
	$ 350,000 Home Value $1,800/month payment +$400 extra

8-1 Case Study (Steve): Background Profile

Steve's Goals

Steve thinks that his income is too high to qualify for financial aid. He doesn't plan on filing a FAFSA because he thinks he makes too much money, but he needs an additional $20,000 to $30,000 per year for the next six years to send his children to a $50,000 per year university (Figure 8-2).

Steve's goals are not out of range for where he's at financially and for the level of students his children are. Nevertheless, Steve still has a $20,000 to $30,000 a year problem.

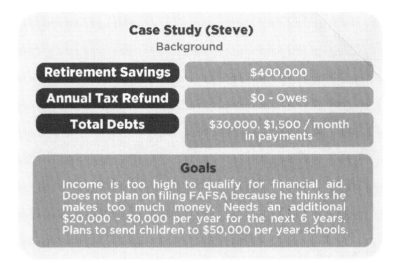

Case Study (Steve)
Background

Retirement Savings	$400,000
Annual Tax Refund	$0 - Owes
Total Debts	$30,000, $1,500 / month in payments

Goals

Income is too high to qualify for financial aid. Does not plan on filing FAFSA because he thinks he makes too much money. Needs an additional $20,000 - 30,000 per year for the next 6 years. Plans to send children to $50,000 per year schools.

8-2 Case Study (Steve): Background and Goals

If we examine only the fixed expenses, his mortgage is $2,200 a month; he's adding $2,000 a month into his 401(k) and $300 a month into mutual funds. He is not adding to the bank savings. He is paying $1,200 per month toward his credit card debt of $18,000. His total fixed expenses are about $5,700, which is very manageable for someone at his income level (Figure 8-3).

There are other fixed expenses as well as variable expenses such as taxes, health insurance, food, vacations, school activities, sports, dance, automobile insurance, and much more, but we will focus on the expenses that have an impact on college.

Case Study (Steve)
Background

Basic Lifestyle Family: 2 Children, $250,000 Salary		Monthly Payment
Home Value	$ 350,000	
Mortgage Balance	150,000	$ 2,200
Home Equity Value	200,000	
401 (k) Balance	400,000	2,000
Mutual Funds	250,000	300
Bank Savings	40,000	0
Average Annual Tax Refund	0	0
Credit Card Debt	18,000	1,200
Monthly Outlay		$5,700

8-3 Case Study (Steve): Background and Monthly Payments

In Figure 8-4 (below), everything that's bold and has an asterisk has a direct effect on Steve's ability to receive gifted money from the universities according to FAFSA.

CASE STUDY #1: STEVE

Case Study (Steve)
Background: Impact on FAFSA/CSS Profile

Basic Lifestyle Family: 2 Children, $250,000 Salary		Monthly Payment
Home Value	$ 350,000	
Mortgage Balance *	150,000	$ 2,200
Home Equity Value *	200,000	
401 (k) Balance *	400,000	2,000
Mutual Funds *	250,000	300
Bank Savings *	40,000	0
Average Annual Tax Refund	0	0
Credit Card Debt	18,000	1,200
Monthly Outlay		$5,700

*Potential impact on FAFSA/CSS Profile

8-4 Case Study (Steve): Background and Impact
on FAFSA/CSS Profile

There are a number of options available to Steve to reduce his college costs, but we will only focus on those areas that have a direct impact on FAFSA and the CSS Profile.

The Mortgage

We will begin by taking a look at the mortgage. Refinancing Steve's balance on his mortgage will reduce his monthly payment from $2,200 to $725, increasing his monthly cash flow by $1,475. Once he submits his last financial aid application for his children, college is no longer a concern and he can go back to accelerating the mortgage payment if he so chooses.

101

Steve has enough money if he absolutely needs it, but when his children are going to school, does he want to borrow $20,000 a year at 6.4%-7.9% or would he rather make a $725 a month tax deductible mortgage payment?

In addition to the extra cash flow, since his children are considering colleges that penalize him for equity in his home, refinancing the home will reduce what he is expected to pay for college and may allow him to qualify for free gifting from the universities. Once he is done with college, he can put everything back in order and he will be in a better position. He became FAFSA Friendly instead of taking out additional loans and being friendly to Sallie Mae.

Funding Your Retirement Without Being Penalized

It is true that the balances in a retirement plan such as a 401(k) or IRA do not count on the FAFSA, but the annual contributions to these plans do. Steve can stop funding his 401(k), but he doesn't have to stop funding his retirement.

Since he is an owner of the company, he has many different options to fund retirement. He can institute a $2,500 per month deferred compensation program instead of the 401(k). A profit sharing plan might do the same thing, but it doesn't help with cash flexibility or future tax issues. Very few colleges will count a deferred compensation plan against you. Schools that do will add that question to the supplemental area of the Profile, and the Profile will list which schools ask about it.

The deferred compensation plan provides him the ability to set more money aside that he can use for his retirement. It also reduces his Adjusted Gross Income (AGI), which saves money in college. He still receives tax advantages on his savings and, when structured properly, he can actually have better tax advantages into the future.

In a nutshell, if you pay less for college, you have less debt and more money in your pocket and can save more for your retirement in a tax-favored fashion, which means less taxes and RMD's (Required Minimum Distributions) during retirement. It's a win-win situation.

If you are a business owner and feel like you are already getting pummeled from Uncle Sam, and do not want to get pummeled from Sallie Mae and FAFSA, consider contacting a college professional who understands the ins and outs of this process.

AHA MOMENT #18

 Business owners, even high-income business owners, can take advantage of opportunities to reduce the cost of college, even during record profit years.

Non-Qualified Accounts

Since he is 55 years old, Steve is allowed to have about $40,000 before FAFSA begins to assess his non-qualified savings accounts. In Steve's case, $210,000 of his $250,000 in mutual funds are counting against him, and he is compounding the problem by adding more money each month. He can still take that $250,000 and invest it, but it needs to be done in a way that is not going to penalize him on FAFSA.

Annuities are one option for him and may work well in his case, but he needs to review his options with a professional to make sure it is the right fit for his family. It is important that whatever the decision, he invests in a way that puts his family and goals first.

If Steve keeps his mutual funds, his kids will graduate from college and his nest egg will be worth less, maybe by $100,000 or more. It would be better to have him protect it and have the full amount working for him for as long as he needs it, instead of allowing Sallie Mae to dictate how to spend it.

You should save in a way that will benefit you first instead of the universities or the government. Protect what you have worked hard for. Do not expose your savings to the FAFSA risk.

AHA MOMENT #19

 Your non-qualified assets, such as stocks and bonds, CDs, savings, checking and money market accounts will add to your emergency fund, yet they will increase your college cost, often adding to the parent loan portion of the financial aid offer from the colleges.

Additional Strategies

Steve can pull money out of his savings and pay off his credit card debt which saves him about $1,200 a month.

He has the ability to contribute to a Flex Spending Account (FSA). By adding $2,400 to an FSA, Steve will benefit from a dollar for dollar reduction in his AGI and reduce his EFC.

8-5 Case Study (Steve): Money Freed up for Tuition

Summing It Up

Remember traditional planning uses your money first, the government's money second and the university's money third. *By making these changes Steve is using the university's money first, the government's money second, and his money last.*

Implementing these changes reduces out-of-pocket monthly expenses from $5,700 to $3,425, adding almost $2,300 a month back in Steve's pocket (Figure 8-5). That is over $27,000 a year. He is well on his way to achieving his goal of an extra $20,000 - $30,000 per year.

These strategies do not require any additional savings or changes in lifestyle. Most important, they are based on knowledge and a strategy, not a product. A 529 did not solve his college problem. When Steve has one child in college, he has extra money, and when both children are in school he has a much smaller problem. When his kids get out of college, he will be in a much better situation than before.

Reducing the EFC

Moving $250,000 of mutual funds into an account that is not assessed on FAFSA will reduce the EFC by about $14,000. By choosing the right strategy (legally, morally and ethically) it can still be invested and accessed, just not counted on the FAFSA. Every family is different, so it is important to evaluate your strategy to ensure it meets the requirements for your situation. You want to be careful with your money and you don't want to create more problems than solutions.

AHA MOMENT #20

The rules and regulations which allow changes are written as part of the FAFSA and law. Your assets and income change on an annual basis, so it is important to have a strategy that is flexible enough to work throughout the college years.

Steve's oldest son has $20,000 in his savings which will create a hefty penalty on the FAFSA. Assets owned by the student are assessed a penalty of 20% on the FAFSA. In Steve's case, his son's assets are adding $4,000 to his EFC. This is an additional $4,000 that he is going to overpay because his son has money in savings.

While FAFSA has a previous year look-back on income, assets only have a one-day look-back so there is more flexibility on when to make changes to assets. This money can be used to pay for things his son needs prior to filing the FAFSA or in some cases can be moved to a non-penalized (or less-penalized) account.

Stopping the 401(k) and implementing the deferred compensation program lowered his EFC by about $10,650 a year. Remember, he is a business owner and can do this. If you work for a company that offers this type of savings, it might be a good fit for your family. You should research and plan with your CPA to be sure.

Contributing to the FSA reduces his EFC by $721. If your company offers an FSA (Flex Spending Account), it might be a good fit during the college years or even beyond. You need to be sure to spend all of your contributions during the year or you will lose any remaining balance the next year.

Myth: I Make Too Much Money to Receive Financial Aid

Steve's original EFC at his income level with his assets is $86,633. He is expected to be able to afford $86,633 per year in college expenses, more than ⅓ of his income. On the surface, it appears he won't receive any gifted money for college.

When he has two kids in college at the same time, he will have a total of $100,000 per year cost of attendance. The FAFSA says he has the ability to pay $86,633, and the schools will help him with about $14,000. But, by making the right changes, Steve can reduce his EFC from $86,633 to $57,159 (Figure 8-6). During those years with two kids attending high-gifting colleges, his family could receive almost $40,000 a year in financial aid!

Steve's kids will not receive any needs-based assistance when only one child is in school because his EFC is higher than the cost of attendance of a $50,000 school. During the years he has two children in school, his EFC will drop to about $29,000 per child, $21,000 below the cost of attendance at the schools they are targeting. The colleges he chooses then have the ability to gift that amount, per child.

Choosing schools that offer higher needs-based gifting percentages will allow him to get more free money. Choosing schools that offer lower needs-based gifting will increase the amount of parent loans he has to take. Most private colleges gift at a much higher rate than the public colleges. Despite having a higher sticker price than the public colleges, most private colleges will provide higher levels of gifting which will tend to bring their out-of-pocket cost more in line with public colleges, and sometimes even lower.

Private colleges can provide more gifting because they typically have larger endowment funds to work with but, just as importantly, private colleges are not as highly regulated by the state governments as public colleges are. Since public colleges receive so much funding from state governments, their hands are often tied with how they manage their money.

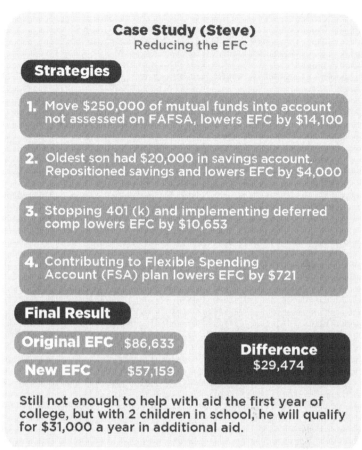

Case Study (Steve)
Reducing the EFC

Strategies

1. Move $250,000 of mutual funds into account not assessed on FAFSA, lowers EFC by $14,100

2. Oldest son had $20,000 in savings account. Repositioned savings and lowers EFC by $4,000

3. Stopping 401 (k) and implementing deferred comp lowers EFC by $10,653

4. Contributing to Flexible Spending Account (FSA) plan lowers EFC by $721

Final Result

Original EFC $86,633

New EFC $57,159

Difference
$29,474

Still not enough to help with aid the first year of college, but with 2 children in school, he will qualify for $31,000 a year in additional aid.

8-6 Case Study (Steve): Strategies to Lower EFC

Steve could take advantage of many more options to reduce his EFC. He can choose to implement the strategies with which his family is comfortable. He can evaluate his options and choose a happy medium that fits his goals and lifestyle.

AHA MOMENT #21

 The traditional financial and tax planning you have been doing is probably going to help you to overpay for college. A different strategy is required during the college years.

Steve's original cost was just under $400,000 over six years. His new cost is $337,888. With two children going to school, if he does nothing, he will pay an extra $62,000 for college. Even at $250,000 a year of income, $62,000 is a substantial amount of savings.

Steve's transferred amount (cash flow increase) is $27,300 per year for a total difference of more than $37,000 including his reduced EFC (Figure 8-7). Factoring in his annual savings over six years, this becomes a $226,000 swing in his family household economy. This is significant because it means there is $226,000 that he doesn't have to spend from his investment accounts, or $226,000 that he doesn't have to borrow in loans at 6.4% - 7.9% interest. Steve is better off controlling his money than letting the FAFSA and Sallie Mae dictate his family's future.

Case Study (Steve)
The Cost of Doing Nothing

Original cost of college
$50,000
($400,000 over 6 years)

New cost of college
$34,472
($337,888 over 6 years)

2 Children over 6 years will cost Steve an additional $62,112 if he makes no changes, plus his student loan amount could increase by an additional $163,800 due to the transfers.

Transferred Amount $27,300

Total Annual Difference $37,652

Total Cost of Doing Nothing: $225,912
Applied Knowledge is Power

8-7 Case Study (Steve): The Cost of Doing Nothing

AHA Moment Recap:

#18 Business owners have more opportunities during the college years that will help reduce parent loans as well as taxes, now and in the future

#19 Your non-qualified money (stocks, bonds, mutual funds, savings, checking, money market accounts) will add to your emergency fund, and that can put your family over the asset threshold limit. You can protect your assets during the college years.

#20 Taking advantage of the FAFSA rules to reduce your out-of-pocket cost for college is no different than using a CPA to reduce your taxes.

#21 Traditional financial planning could be positioning you to OVERPAY for college.

Chapter 9
Case Study #2: Patricia

Our second case study involves Patricia. Patricia is a single mother and works in the automotive industry. She has one son and makes $48,000 a year. She has a mortgage of $55,000 on a 5-year ARM (Adjustable-Rate Mortgage), she has a house worth $120,000 and she's paying $540 a month in payments (Figure 9-1).

Case Study (Patricia)
Background

Client:	Patricia M.
Age:	45
Occupation:	Automotive Industry
Family Status:	Single Parent, one child
Income:	$ 48,000
Mortgage:	$ 55,000 5-year ARM $120,000 Home Value $540/Month Payment

9-1 Case Study (Patricia): Background

Patricia has no retirement savings because the company she works for does not offer a 401(k). She receives an average tax refund of $3,000. She has struggled to make ends meet, and has amassed a total amount of debt of $35,000 between her car and credit cards. She is paying

$900 a month toward her debt, enough to reduce the balances but not enough to pay off her debt in a reasonable amount of time. She has no emergency fund, so when a problem arises it usually gets paid for with a credit card.

Patricia's College Problem

Patricia needs $750 per month to supplement financial aid and tuition assistance programs (Figure 9-2). She wants to send her son to a $25,000-a-year state college which is not out of reach for the level of student her son is. How exactly did she arrive at the $750 per month requirement?

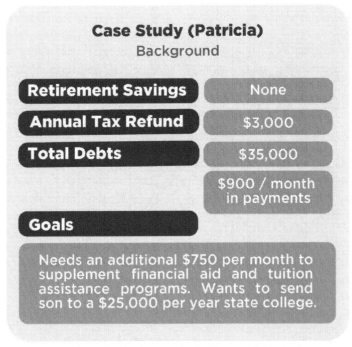

9-2 Case Study (Patricia): Background & Goals

The cost of attendance at the schools Patricia and her son are considering is about $25,000 per year. Her current EFC is $3,686, which she has to pay no matter what. The school will subtract the $3,686 from their cost of $25,000 leaving $21,314. If the school is a 35% gifting college (typical of a large state public college), they will gift 35% of the $21,314 or $7,460. Her new out-of-pocket cost is reduced from $25,000 to $17,540.

If her son takes on average $6,750 per year in student loans, it will reduce her out-of-pocket cost further to $10,790. Her low EFC will probably allow her son to qualify for work-study while in school, so this can reduce her necessary expense another $2,000 requiring $8,790 per year, or $732 per month. She rounded up to $750 for her goal.

Keep in mind that since her EFC is below $5,000 she will qualify for Pell Grant money from the government of about $2,000. This $2,000 will be included as part of the college's award package, so it won't increase her award. The college will just use the government's money instead of their own. However, most colleges will increase the gifting percentage when the EFC falls below a certain level, especially if it is in "Pell Grant territory" so she may qualify for additional financial aid to ease her situation.

Patricia's Current Financial Situation

As we did with the previous case study, we will look only at the fixed expenses. Patricia is paying $540 a month for her mortgage. She is not adding to her retirement or bank savings. She is actually loaning Uncle Sam $250 a month because her withholding at work is set up to overpay on her taxes by $3,000 a year. Her car payment of $250 and credit card payments of $650 per month total the amount she pays toward her debt.

An interesting thing occurred in Patricia's life. Her mother recently passed away, and she received an inheritance of a $250,000 home, $80,000 cash to her, and $20,000 cash for her son. Do you see any FAFSA red flags?

Patricia's total monthly outlay is almost $1,700 (Figure 9-3). This is not out of range for her income, but she is not making any headway to save for college or retirement. The inheritance will certainly help, but as you will see, it could also be gone in a flash if she is forced to use it to pay for college.

Case Study (Patricia)
Background

Basic Lifestyle Family: 1 Child, $50,000 Salary		Monthly Payment
Home Value	$ 120,000	
Mortgage Balance	55,000	$ 540
Home Equity Value	65,000	
401 (k) Balance	0	0
Mutual Funds	0	0
Bank Savings	3,000	0
Average Annual Tax Refund	3,000	250
Credit Card Debt	25,000	650
Car Debt	10,000	250
Inheritance: $250,000 Home / $ 80,000 / Cash $20,000 for son		
Monthly Outlay		$ 1,690

9-3 Case Study (Patricia): Background & Monthly Payments

College is only a couple of years away for Patricia, so it needs to be the primary focus for now. Once a college plan is put in place, a retirement plan will be established. Take note of a key interpretation of this statement. Retirement savings will begin after the college PLAN is set up, not after college is PAID FOR. Time is a critical factor for saving for retirement, so it needs to begin as soon as possible.

The first step for Patricia is to refinance her house. Unlike Steve, Patricia will pull additional money out of the home to help pay down her debt. If she can earn more by investing her inheritance money instead of using it to pay down the 4% interest rate on her mortgage, it might make sense to use the home equity to pay down the debt. This debt may be costing her 14% - 29% per year, depending on the credit card, and it is tax deductible.

Even though she is refinancing a higher balance than before, changing to a 30-year fixed mortgage will actually reduce her monthly payments by $110 because she can qualify for a lower interest rate. The fixed period on her Adjustable Rate Mortgage (ARM) has expired and her monthly payments have gone up substantially due to increased interest rates. Regardless of whether she is planning for college, she needs to do something about the ARM and move into a fixed rate mortgage to give her better control over her money. By refinancing the home, she can pay off her debt and reduce her combined monthly payments by $960 (Figure 9-4).

Case Study (Patricia)
Result

Lifestyle				
	Value	Old Monthly Payment	New Monthly Payment	Recaptured Transfers
Home Value	$ 120,000			
Mortgage Balance *	90,000	$ 540	$ 430	$ 110
Home Equity Value *	30,000			
401 (k) *	0	0	0	
Mutual Funds *	0	0	200	-200
Bank Savings *	3,000	0	100	-100
Annual Tax Refund	3,000	250	0	250
Credit Card Debt	25,000	650	0	650
Car Debt	10,000	250	0	250
Monthly Outlay		$ 1,690	$ 730	$ 960
Money freed up for tuition:			**$11,520/year**	

*Potential impact on FAFSA/CSS Profile

9-4: Case Study (Patricia): Money Freed up for Tuition

As a side note, many traditional planners and radio personalities will tell you to pay off the mortgage and save the interest. That might be a good strategy if you do not have college on the horizon. However, in this case and many others, the money used for the mortgage and other debt will be replaced with a parent loan that comes with a 6.4 – 7.9% interest rate with an additional origination fee that can be as high as 4%. During the college years we need to think differently about how our money works.

Patricia can't participate in a 401(k) at her work but she can create a personal savings program. She can start small by adding $200 a month to a mutual fund or another investment account. This could grow to over $160,000 by the time she retires. It's not enough to retire on, but it's a start. When her son graduates from college she can increase her contributions in order to secure her retirement income.

Patricia will also begin adding $100 a month into a bank savings account to create a small emergency fund in order to prevent her from getting into debt again. The safety net will be there for her if the tire blows, her son's shoes need to be replaced or she needs to purchase a new dishwasher. It is very important to set up a strategy that keeps Patricia in control of her finances.

You may be thinking that adding money into non-qualified accounts will put Patricia in danger of increasing her EFC, and you would be right. However, setting up some type of retirement program is essential to proper planning, and you will see later that, in her particular case, the extra savings will not impact her EFC.

Making these changes lowers her expenses from $1,690 to $730 a month, adding $960 a month back in her pocket. Remember, her monthly college goal is $750. She has solved her college problem using a strategy, not a traditional product-based solution.

The "FAIR" Application for Federal Student Aid

You may think that all is sunny in Patricia's household, but she still has that elephant in the room, the inheritance problem. Her recent inheritance could increase her EFC from $3,686 to $23,871 per year. The second home adds $250,000 to her assets and she has to tend with the $20,000 in her son's name. She is well above her asset threshold, and her parents' desire to help make her life better will actually eat away at their intended legacy.

It is now FAFSA's turn to rub some salt in the wound, as it often does. A two-parent family with a 45-year-old is allowed to have about $30,700 in savings. Yet Patricia is a single parent, so she is only allowed to have $7,100 in savings before she is penalized (Figure 9-

5). Remember that apparently FAFSA thinks that if you live on one income and you get injured or lose your job, you don't need as much savings as a two-parent family.

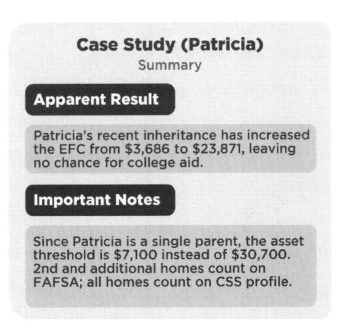

Case Study (Patricia)
Summary

Apparent Result

Patricia's recent inheritance has increased the EFC from $3,686 to $23,871, leaving no chance for college aid.

Important Notes

Since Patricia is a single parent, the asset threshold is $7,100 instead of $30,700. 2nd and additional homes count on FAFSA; all homes count on CSS profile.

9-5: Case Study (Patricia): Summary

To make matters worse, the public is slowly being squeezed by the government to qualify for less financial aid. Over the last several years the asset threshold limits have been going down, which means you are allowed less savings before you are penalized with a higher EFC.

In 2015, a household with two parents, the oldest being 45 years old, was allowed to have $30,700 before penalties kicked in. In 2010, that number was $46,600. For a single parent household with the same age, in 2015, the allowance was $7,100. In 2010, it was $18,300, 258% higher than in 2015! It is the Free Application for Federal

Student Aid, not the "FAIR" Application for Federal Student Aid. There is nothing fair about it.

The Saving Grace – a FAFSA Loophole

Now, here is what's interesting. Since Patricia makes under $50,000 a year, and she meets one additional criteria on the FAFSA, she's eligible for the Simplified FAFSA, and *none of her assets count*. The additional criteria can be one of several options.

1. The student has qualified for free or reduced lunch in high school sometime during the previous two years.
2. The parents have qualified for any of several federal benefit programs, including WIC, SNAP, SSI or TANF.
3. The parents are eligible to file a 1040A or 1040EZ tax form. They don't have to actually file one of these forms, they just have to be eligible. Business owners are typically not eligible. Check with your tax accountant.
4. One of the student's parents is a dislocated worker.

Patricia meets the third criteria, the ability to use IRS Form 1040A to file her taxes, so she currently qualifies for the Simplified FAFSA. Patricia is at the $48,000 mark for her Adjusted Gross Income, which is just under the threshold.

Implementing the right strategy can save her thousands per year on college, but she needs to be careful. Since she works in the automotive industry, in Michigan, when they hit busy season during model changeover, they have a few weeks to get a lot done and they typically work overtime. She could easily earn an extra $2,000 in overtime which would put her over the $50,000 limit, increasing her EFC by over $20,000.

Patricia needs to inform her supervisor at work of her situation and explain why she doesn't want to take the extra overtime, so she doesn't fall into the category of a non-team player. If her income does climb above $50,000, as long as she is aware of the FAFSA rules she can plan for that and other strategies can be implemented to prevent her from overpaying for college.

By controlling her income, being aware of the FAFSA Rules, and becoming FAFSA Friendly, she can maintain control of her money and actually save a lot of money for college.

If Patricia does nothing, one student over four years will cost her an extra $36,000 in loans. If her income climbs above $50,000, the loans will be substantially higher. She will not have the ability to pay for it. By making these changes, she has enough money to pay for college and improve her lifestyle.

AHA MOMENT #22

 FAFSA requires every college to penalize you for equity in second and additional homes.

AHA MOMENT #23

 If not planned carefully, an inheritance designed to help your family during the college years could actually take you out of the running for gift money from the university your child wants to attend.

Your Financial Team

Most people have some type of financial team they rely on to help them with their financial goals in life. Their financial team can consist of a financial planner, stockbroker, life insurance agent, banker, etc. All of these people work to help with life's financial hurdles. How is your team assembled? Are you even aware that you have a team?

Most people do not interview their team or make sure that everyone is on the same page, or has the same philosophy, resulting in additional stress in their lives. The people on your financial team are the people that you rely on to help you meet your financial goals in life. They are the experts in areas that you do not have time to learn about and understand.

The professionals on a family's financial team will usually vary from family to family (Figure 9-6). If you are proactive with your financial planning, your team may consist of a mortgage broker, CPA, estate planning attorney, life insurance agent, financial planner, home and auto agent, banker and hopefully a college planner. The problem is, you have eight different people functioning in your life, they each have an agenda and right now, when it comes to college, it's not you (except for the college planner of course).

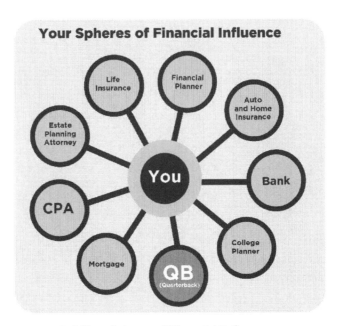

9-6 Your Spheres of Financial Influence

You need someone to enter the picture and play quarterback. During the years leading up to and during college, a college planner can help with this process. A very small percentage of CPA's or financial planners understand exactly how the college game works.

A college planner can let you know how much you should put in your 401(k) to avoid overpaying for college, and explain to your CPA the reasons for doing so. This will help your CPA understand that you are not just looking at a 12-month tax deduction, or tax refund, but are instead looking at how the funding of your retirement will actually cost you more for college than save you in taxes. Your CPA is then provided with enough information to make an educated decision based on facts.

A quarterback can help you talk with your financial advisor, who will have a temper tantrum because you are not funding his future, and explain the benefit of making changes from a college perspective. That is a joke, of course, and no one likes to lose business, but providing accurate information to your financial advisor can set him at ease knowing that you are in the best position possible for the long run. Remember, once the college process is completed, everything can be put back the way it was before.

A quarterback can talk to your mortgage person and explain why she should place you in a 30-year fixed mortgage instead of accelerating it over 15 years with bi-weekly payments. She can understand why paying the mortgage off right before the kids enter college will penalize your family more in college tuition than what you pay in interest. Remember the mortgage calculations. Why do you want to pay off a mortgage at 4.5% tax deductible interest and start accruing a 6.4-7.9% non-tax deductible parent loan? You need someone in your corner so that, for the first time, you have an agenda that works with all the pieces of the puzzle, and it is centered around YOUR FAMILY.

Chapter 10
How Colleges Determine Your Ability to Pay for Tuition

The Old College Two-Step

How do the colleges determine your ability to get money? It is a two-step process. We spent the first part of this book discussing how to reduce your Expected Family Contribution (EFC). We will now focus on Step Two, finding the schools which offer the most free money. If you reduce your EFC and only apply to schools that don't give money away, you are not going to get any free money. You will only get stuck with high-interest loans.

You will see from the following example that quite often the school with the lower sticker cost is more expensive because they have different gifting formulas.

The size of your financial aid award is determined by your FAFSA score, how well you control your cost, and how you take advantage of the opportunities that are within your family economy. It then becomes a matter of finding the colleges with the highest gifting formulas that meet your child's criteria for a major and an academic level that fits his style.

Let's consider two types of schools, one low-cost public and an expensive private college. We will assume the family has an EFC of $5,000. We will also assume the student is qualified to be accepted to both colleges.

The private college has a list price of $63,000 while the price of the public college is $21,000. From a financial point of view, it would appear that in this case the public college is the obvious bargain, but remember, these are list prices and not what you actually pay. The number you must ultimately focus on is your out-of-pocket cost, not the advertised price.

To calculate your out-of-pocket cost, the schools will subtract your EFC of $5,000 from the list price. They will then meet a percentage of that difference with free, gifted money. If you subtract the EFC from the list price, you are left with $58,000 for the private college and $16,000 for the public college. This is your financial need; the number that is used to calculate your needs-based assistance. Public colleges will almost always meet a much lower percentage of the financial need than private colleges.

In this case, the public college meets 21% of the financial need so they will gift you $3,400. The private college, on the other hand, will meet a much higher 88% of your financial need, so they will gift you $51,000. You calculate your out-of-pocket cost by subtracting the gifting from the list price (Figure 10-1). It's that simple.

Actual vs. Advertised Cost
Hypothetical Example

Private College		Public College	
Cost	$63,000	Cost	$21,000
EFC	5,000	EFC	5,000
Need	58,000	Need	16,000
% of Need Met	88%	% of Need Met	21%
School Gifting	51,000	School Gifting	3,400
Savings, Loans, Work - Study	7,000	Savings, Loans, Work - Study	12,600
Cost to Parents / Student	$12,000	Cost to Parents / Student	$17,600

10-1 Private vs Public College Cost: Actual vs Advertised

In this case, your out-of-pocket cost is $17,600 for the public college and $12,000 for the private college. Now, which school do you want your child to attend? Do you want to pay $17,600 a year for a $21,000 per year school, or do you want to pay $12,000 a year for a $63,000 per year school?

If your EFC is higher than $5,000, you will certainly pay more for college. It is important to remember that there are thousands of colleges in this country, all with different gifting percentages, and you have an opportunity to consider colleges based on the best fit for the student, not just on list price. Calculating your true out-of-pocket cost is a critical part of your college strategy (Figure 10-2).

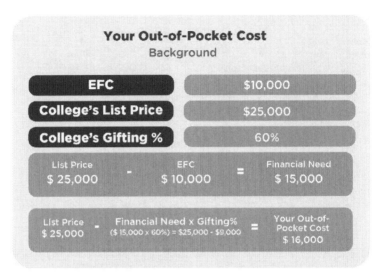

Your Out-of-Pocket Cost
Background

EFC	$10,000
College's List Price	$25,000
College's Gifting %	60%

List Price	-	EFC	=	Financial Need
$ 25,000		$ 10,000		$ 15,000

List Price	-	Financial Need x Gifting%	=	Your Out-of-Pocket Cost
$ 25,000		($ 15,000 x 60%) = $25,000 - $9,000		$ 16,000

10-2 Calculating Your Out-of-Pocket Cost

You need to ensure you have the correct information. Not all the information on the Internet is accurate, and some schools don't always gift at the same percentages as what is advertised. There have been trends over the last few years in which colleges provide a higher percentage of gifting to lower income families. Public colleges will almost always gift at a lower percentage for out-of-state students than in-state residents. Ensure you have a reliable source of information on these trends so you can prepare in the best way possible.

AHA MOMENT #24

Every college will gift at a different level. It should be a critical part of your family's strategy, especially if you have more than one child.

Where Does the Money Come From?

College financial aid is available from five basic sources, comprised of grants, scholarships, loans, tax deductions and work study (Figure 10-3).

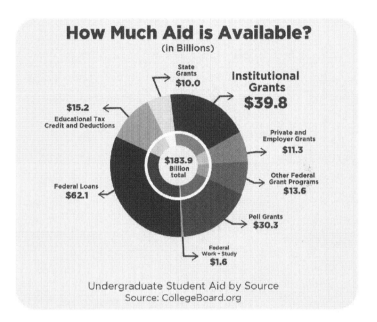

How Much Aid is Available?
(in Billions)

State Grants **$10.0**

Institutional Grants $39.8

$15.2 Educational Tax Credit and Deductions

Private and Employer Grants **$11.3**

$183.9 Billion total

Other Federal Grant Programs **$13.6**

Federal Loans **$62.1**

Pell Grants **$30.3**

Federal Work - Study **$1.6**

Undergraduate Student Aid by Source
Source: CollegeBoard.org

10-3 How Much Aid is Available?

Grants actually make up the largest portion of college aid, second to loans. Grants come in many flavors. They can be from the federal and state governments, private employers and the colleges themselves (institutional grants). Institutional Grants from the colleges come in the form of gift aid, and make up about 22% of the total financial aid available.

Institutional Grants are a big piece of the pie and the part that is most easily attained by choosing the right colleges based on your EFC and the gifting percentage of the colleges. Federal loans, that wonderful piece of the pie that continues to add to the $1.3 trillion in college loan debt, make up 34% of the total financial aid provided each year.

Other types of aid include work-study. Work-study is a federal program that allows the student to work on campus during the school year. The jobs are supposed to allow for some down time so the student can study when not doing a task. The average work-study awards are $2,200 per year, but can be as high as $3,500. When you fill out the FAFSA, check "Yes" to work study. It provides your children the opportunity to be first in line for jobs on campus.

One benefit to work-study is that the FAFSA will not count those earnings on your EFC. The student will have to pay taxes, but FAFSA asks how much work-study was earned and then subtracts that amount from the student's income. Students are paid directly and can use the funds to pay for tuition and incidentals while attending college.

Some families are hesitant to allow their kids to participate in work-study. They think that college is a big enough change. They are worried about their kids adjusting to having a roommate, remembering where they parked the bicycle, finding the classrooms, figuring out the cafeteria, etc. Parents, don't fall into this trap. Stand your ground and encourage your kids to take work study, if it is offered.

Studies have shown that students who have a job on campus, first semester of the freshmen year, have higher grades than those who don't. Consider that every dollar the student makes is a dollar less you have to give them for incidentals. This reduces your cost and your loan package.

Other Money

We have covered loans and gifting as sources for financial aid, but what about outside sources? Outside sources are people or places you know that might provide money.

One example of an outside source goes like this, "Honey, we have to spend $5,000 for a down payment on college in the next two weeks and we're going to go see grandma right now. Turn your tears on so we can ask for some money."

If you have the ability to leverage that, use it. However, there is a downside. You might find that every year between July and September, Grandma and Grandpa take a two-month vacation and avoid the teary-eyed conversation. If you don't have that opportunity to leverage an outside source of money, then you have to play in the same sandbox as everyone else.

Harvard has often been called the most affordable college in the country. This is a strange statement considering that their list price in 2015 was $69,900. It looks eerily similar to a sales tag at the local home goods store. $9.99, $19.99, $59.95, except in this case it is a college education that is on sale.

Well, in Harvard's case, this is actually true. Harvard's gifting formula states they will meet 93% of the difference between your EFC and their list price. A family with a $12,000 EFC will pay about $16,000 a year for an education at Harvard. If you let the kids pick up the full $27,000 of student loans, then mom and dad are out a total of only $37,000 for four years of education. And four years it will most likely be—86% of students graduate Harvard within four years.

Top colleges try very hard to get their students off campus and into the job market within four years. Harvard gives away more than $160 million of financial aid each year. You may wonder how they can afford that. They just happen to have the third largest endowment fund in the world at a value of $35.6 billion.

Don't think you have to send your kids to Harvard to get a large discount on college. There are many colleges all over the country with good gifting percentages and good four-year graduation rates. While it is true that in general, private colleges gift more money than public colleges, there are still many public colleges around the country who are generous with their money for need-based assistance. The University of Michigan, University of North Carolina Chapel Hill, University of Virginia and University of Florida are just a few.

 AHA Moment Recap:

#22 Equity in a second and additional homes will increase your EFC.

#23 If not planned properly, an inheritance may increase your EFC so much it takes you out of the running for gifted money from the colleges and the government.

#24 Every college has a different gifting formula that should be accounted for when determining the amount of financial aid you will receive, especially if you have more than one child in college at a time.

Chapter 11

College Strategies

The college game has changed a lot since the late 1970's. Most parents today who have children getting ready to enter college attended college themselves around that time frame. Many of them think because they made it through college that their children can make it through college as well.

The problem is today's college world is much different. You can't get a summer job to pay for next year's tuition. You can't work enough overtime to pay for your child's tuition next year. You can't borrow from your retirement without paying a huge retirement penalty. Your kids cannot borrow all the money they need to pay for their college education. Parents must have an active financial role in today's college game.

The college admissions process has become increasingly competitive. The number of applications has soared. Ivy League colleges consistently receive 30,000 to 40,000 applications per year, only to offer acceptance letters to about 3,000 students. UCLA received a record 112,000 applications for the 2015-2016 school year, the highest in the nation.

Applications from international students are on the rise, but part of the reason is that modern technology has made it easy to apply to college. The increased popularity of the Common App makes it easier than ever to apply to several colleges at once. Unlike the 1970's, you are no longer just competing with the kids in your hometown for the spots available to go to college.

It is so competitive that many college admissions counselors advise prospective students not to tell any of their friends where they are applying to college. Most high-level colleges accept a maximum of two to three students from any one high school, so it is advised to keep quiet so your friends don't apply to the same colleges.

Colleges are a business. They are not just shopping for kids in their own backyards. Colleges look for applicants who will provide lifetime profitability to the university. The colleges are looking to add alumni in every part of the country and market to them for lifetime donations, recognition and marketing dollars.

If your children are looking at the more prestigious schools, they will be required to sell themselves well. It will require more than just good grades to receive those treasured acceptance letters. Because of this, there is a different set of rules or qualifications in order to set the stage to get the "good" money from the university.

The College Timeline

Your college planning process does not start during the senior year in high school! The college game begins, at the latest, by the freshman year in high school, and in some cases as early as grade school. Did your child stick with boy or girl scouts? Did she take her grades seriously during the first semester of her freshman year? Did she sign up for the AP or IB curriculum?

What is she doing during the summer? Is she attending camps at the colleges she wants to attend? Has she reached out to the music instructor, sports person, DECA or robotics team at a specific university? Has she shadowed a professional in her field of interest and interviewed him? Has she done any clinical research in the medical field at the university she would like to attend? The list goes on and on.

Most parents who attended college in the 1970's and 1980's never had to think about any of this. The only thing they were told was to save as much as they could and do well on the ACT or SAT. Beginning in the 1990's when they started having children, the only thing they were told was to save as much as possible for college because by the time the kids get to college it will cost over $100,000 for a college education.

Pre-paid plans, first introduced by Michigan in 1986, and 529 plans, first included in the IRS tax code in 1997, were all the rage, and the public dumped billions of dollars into those plans. The public was given the right advice about one thing, that a college education would cost more than $100,000, but once again, the traditional thought process produced outdated and ineffective conversations. Families desperately need better information.

The reason all of this is so important is that you need to set the stage to be able to leverage the college process in your favor. You may remember from an earlier example that in some cases it is possible to negotiate your college award.

If you go to the car dealership and the car dealer knows you are only looking in one place, are you going to get the best offer? Most of the time you're going to get offered the sticker price and then it is up to you and your ability to negotiate the best deal. How do you negotiate without having another offer?

From the college perspective, your kids need to use the relationships that they created from being active since the freshman year of high school to get colleges competing for them. You have to have the right colleges on the list to which they can apply. You have to communicate with the colleges appropriately so that you can ask for money and reduce your out-of-pocket cost of college.

Not every college will negotiate, but many will. It is not as common for state-funded public universities to negotiate, but some will. They are more receptive if you have a lower EFC. The real opportunities generally arise with mid to high-level private colleges that typically compete with one another.

AHA MOMENT #25

 Some colleges will negotiate with your family. Are you positioned to negotiate and do you have negotiation-friendly colleges on your list?

When you get the award letters in March-April of the high school senior year, they should be reviewed carefully against the schools' gifting percentages. Some schools misaward (make an error unintentionally), some schools under-award and some schools will compete with other colleges.

Notre Dame is not going to compete with Indiana University, but they might compete with Northwestern, Cornell or University of Chicago. They might compete with Vanderbilt or some of the Ivy Leagues. If you want to negotiate between colleges, it is important to do your research by picking the right schools and crafting a well-written appeal letter.

When Does the Negotiation Process Begin?

If you have a high school senior you have until December 31st to position yourself financially before filing the FAFSA starting January 1st. Many of the factors that impact your EFC have no look-back period, meaning you can change them up to one day before you file, but some do. Your FAFSA information must be accurate the day you file. Any changes to your assets need only be completed by the day before you file.

Income, on the other hand, is taken from the previous year. If you have the ability to reduce your Adjusted Gross Income, that strategy used to begin January 1 of the student's junior year in high school. However, in 2015 a directive was issued to change the FAFSA filing dates.

Beginning with the 2017-2018 school year, parents are allowed to file the FAFSA as early as October 1, 2016. Although the new rules allow three additional months to file the FAFSA, the process has become even more confusing and complicated. The previous rules required parents to use the prior year's income on the FAFSA. The new rules require parents to use what is termed as "prior prior" year income. Confused yet?

If the FAFSA is filed in October of the student's senior year in high school, income will count from the calendar year beginning January 1 of the student's sophomore year. This could work for or against you. If your income is lower in the sophomore year in high school, it will work in your favor. If your income is higher during this year it will work against you. In either case, you must implement any strategies to reduce your assessable income a year earlier than before.

What should you do if you find yourself filing a FAFSA with higher income than you currently have? Perhaps you have lost your job or been forced to take a cut in pay. You should notify the financial aid officers at the colleges to which the student applied that you have experienced a reduction in income as soon as possible. Try to contact them before the FAFSA priority filing deadline.

Students can have an overwhelming amount of work to do the last couple of years before starting college, keeping up their GPA and ACT/SAT scores, meeting deadlines and much more.

Parents also have their own homework to do by ensuring their financial house is in order for college. If you only let the kids focus on their responsibilities for preparing for college, you will most likely end up overpaying, or worse, you will have to break the bad news that you just can't afford your daughter's top choice for college.

AHA MOMENT #26

 You will overpay for college if you are not structuring your finances to be FAFSA Friendly and efficient. How much is your traditional structure going to cost your family in parent loans?

Parents, it's Perfectly OK to be Selfish

We are all taught to be generous and to think of others first. One time it is okay to be selfish is when planning how to pay for college. The most a student can receive in direct government loans the first year is $5,500. If the cost of college is over $5,500 per year, and the EFC is higher than that, then you, the parent, will benefit the most from reducing your EFC.

By reducing your EFC, and finding better gifting schools and negotiating, you are not just reducing the cost of college, but you are actually reducing the amount of parent loans you will take. This means that your children can help with the first $5,500 of the first year of college by taking student loans. This will reduce the total college bill for the parents and allow the kids to have some skin in the game.

AHA MOMENT #27

 Not being FAFSA Friendly will add to the PARENT LOAN portion of the financial aid package.

The second thing you have to do is have your children apply to multiple colleges. If your kids apply to only one school, they are locked into only one offer. In order to receive a financial aid offer from a school, you must complete the FAFSA, listing all schools that will receive your financial information.

Financial Aid Officers (FAO) at colleges have unfettered access to all the details of your FAFSA. Since the FAO's can see the schools that are listed on the FAFSA, they will know if you have only applied to one college. If only one college is on the FAFSA, that means one offer will be made, and one offer means no competition and no way to leverage yourself for a better offer. Note: Beginning in the 2017-2018 school year, the FAFSA will block the colleges' ability to see other colleges on the FAFSA.

Including multiple colleges in the application process is a sound strategy even without consideration of the financial aspects. Of course, there is no guarantee your child will get accepted by the schools to which he has applied, but you should always include multiple schools as part of the application process as well as on the FAFSA.

Your Negotiations Begin with the College Selection Process

You can't negotiate if you don't position yourself to ask.

Often times children will say, "I'm not applying to that school, I have no interest in it."

However, adding more schools to the application adds more competition. Offers from colleges that are not as high on your list can still be used as leverage to get a better offer from the top choice schools.

AHA MOMENT #28

 Many colleges will compete with each other by offering more financial aid. Do you have competitive colleges on your list?

When Do You Begin to Position Yourself?

The process for receiving a good financial aid award begins sooner than most people think. You need to position yourself during the application process, the college selection process and as your kids decide in which area they want to study.

The department head for the major of the college your kids will attend will review their application to determine whether they will be accepted into the program. The admissions person will review their credentials for acceptance into the university. The financial aid officer will review your finances to determine how much money will be awarded. All of these people will play a part in the big picture financial strategies that need to happen, and it will help to communicate with all of them.

Each time your child communicates with the college they gain traction. The person who communicates with them can also make a difference. It can be beneficial for the student to maintain communication with the admissions department as well as the department head for the major. Parents can communicate with the financial aid department.

Whenever the student handles a portion of the communication, it lets the college know the student is mature enough to take initiative. It also helps the people at the college get to know the student a little bit better than before. It is a good idea to always get the person's name from the college and speak with that person each time because he will be familiar with your case.

Grade School and Newborns - Not Too Early to Start Planning!

Obviously, you can't begin targeting colleges the day a child is born. It is impossible to know what kind of student a newborn will turn out to be, what her interests will be, or (gasp!) if she will even attend college. A college that is highly ranked today may not be so highly ranked tomorrow. Yet you can start by positioning yourself to save in the best way possible, even before your children are born.

The savings strategies you choose will have a dramatic impact on how well you are positioned to receive as much financial aid as possible, so it is important to save in a way that you won't be penalized by FAFSA. The more you save, the better off you will be, but make sure it is saved in a way that benefits your family first and not FAFSA or Sallie Mae. It is important to learn how the game is played and be responsible to your family first. Work to reduce the amount of college debt you will have and play the game to win.

What is the Best Way to Save for College?

Everyone would like to have a savings strategy that works from grade school through college because they want to set money aside and be responsible. It is crucial that you be responsible for yourself first so when your children go to college, you're not penalized and you have left all your assets on the kitchen table for everyone to see. You have to protect the hard-earned money that you have dedicated to pay for college.

Save in a way that allows you to use the college and government money first and your money last. By implementing a sound strategy, you might actually have extra money in your college fund by the time your children graduate, which can be used for retirement, vacations, graduate school, a wedding or any of life's other financial hurdles.

Whether you are a business owner, W-2 employee or unemployed single-parent, a strategy can be put in place that will work for you. There are options for everyone. Business owners and executives have flexibility on how they take their income. W-2 employees can control how they save so they are not penalized for college. Low-income families have tremendous opportunities for colleges as long as the right schools are chosen during the application process.

The best way to start saving for college is to put a plan in place now. Don't delay the process. Even if you have saved in the wrong way, you may be able to correct it before completing the FAFSA. Beware of overfunding your 401(k) above the employer match. Try to avoid putting money in the student's name, such as UGMA's or UTMA's. Consider alternatives to 529's or similar college plans. A certified college planner can help you determine the best way to save for college so you are not penalized when applying for financial aid.

To find a certified College Specialist, visit College Tuition Checkup at www.FAFSACheck.com and fill out your personal assessment. A locally-trained specialist will email your personal overview and make time available to answer questions about your personal plan. He or she will be able to help guide the process, and provide it as a free benefit to your family.

Broadening the College Search

We just discussed a bit about broadening the college searches. Choosing the best college is not just about the 15 public universities in your state. It is about finding the best schools that fit your children's GPA, test scores, field of study and many others.

How do you choose a college? By looking where your children's friends are going? By where you went? By the sticker price of the college? The distance from your home? These are all important factors. It is very important that the students own the process. The student must find a school that fits his or her needs. This doesn't mean that the parents aren't involved, but the students must be responsible.

The size of the school, the level of diversity, whether the school has religious affiliations or whether it is a party school – all of these factors are important in determining the school that is the best fit for your children. It will help if the student starts with 10 to 15 colleges, and narrows the search from there.

Campus visits are extremely important. Quite frequently, a student sets foot on a campus and immediately knows it is not the school for him. The opposite is also true. Schedule campus visits when the college is in session so that the student can get an idea of the culture of the college. Eat lunch in the cafeteria. Attend some classes if time allows.

Choosing the best college that is the best fit for the student is an often overlooked strategy. One of the most expensive ways to attend college is to transfer schools in the middle of the process. Transferring schools will lengthen the time it takes to graduate and cost more money. Remember that government loans are only available to undergraduates for four and a half years. After that, the parents will usually bear the burden of financial responsibility.

Do not forget to look at the graduation rates for the colleges on your list. Schools that average a four and a half-year graduation rate will work harder to get your kids out of school than those with six-year graduation rates. When you lengthen the time in college, it also lengthens the time before the student is in the work force, adding an even greater cost to the problem.

Many larger universities will utilize a TA (teaching assistant) or GA (grad-assistant) to lead some of the classes. Sometimes English is not their primary language. Will your child thrive in that environment, or will he be better taught by a professor who has connections in the field he wants to work in and can help get internships, share real world experiences, and is interested in helping your child? Do you want your child to only be a number, or be a person with a name and a face? Do you want your children recognized by the professor and taught by a professor or just be part of a 300-person class taught by a TA?

Students can have either experience at large and small colleges, so size is not the determining factor. The culture of the school is the determining factor.

 AHA Moment Recap:

#25 Not every college will negotiate your award. Choose colleges for your list that are negotiation-friendly.

#26 You can manage your finances to become FAFSA Friendly. Do not give money away by not being FAFSA-efficient!

#27 Every reduced EFC dollar saves the parents loans, and being FAFSA Friendly saves the parents money!

#28 Colleges will compete. Make sure the colleges on your list are the right colleges for these strategies.

No More $20,000 Experiments

Students commonly choose colleges that their friends attend. While that can certainly be one of the reasons, it should never be the final determining factor. Homework needs to be done so informed choices can be made. Otherwise, college just becomes a $20,000 experiment. If you are looking at a $20,000 experiment, then perhaps community college would be a better choice for a year or two until a better decision can be made. This all comes back to having a strategy for college. Don't just try to figure it out.

AHA MOMENT #29

 Reducing the cost of college starts now, not once you are in college. Determining your starting point helps uncover your opportunities.

AHA MOMENT #30

 Every family has several ways to save money on college. They all require some work, but getting started will set the stage for maximum savings.

 AHA Moment Recap:

#29 You can start the college cost reduction journey at any time. It is NEVER too late or too early to begin.

#30 There are several areas that every family has in common. Every family has a different starting point, where should you start?

Chapter 12
Getting Started

Change. Open-mindedness. Resolve. These are all characteristics you need to formulate and implement a successful college plan. Unless you are a part of the one percent of the population who have already assembled the perfect college plan, you will need to make some changes in order to improve the situation for your family.

Some strategies that will put you in a better position will fly directly in the face of what you may have known about college before reading this book. You may feel like you've been drinking from a fire hose while trying to absorb a lot of information all at once. That's okay. Take a couple of deep breaths, regroup, and wake up in the morning with an open mind ready to implement the strategy that is best for your family, regardless of your past thought process. Finally, resolve yourself to develop a college strategy and stick to it through completion.

Once you decide to design a strategy, get your financial house in order. This doesn't mean to pay off your debt, save $20,000, and wait until your daughter has finalized her decision on which college she will attend. You need to start now before it is too late.

Get your financial house in order by gathering your financial information together so you can calculate your overall cost for college. Grab your last completed tax return and your W-2's. Determine the value of your home(s), and write down how much you owe so you can calculate the amount of equity. Write down the balances in your financial accounts including your checking, savings, brokerage, CD, IRA, college savings and others. Write down the balances in the accounts your children own. Having all this information at hand will allow you to calculate your EFC and your baseline out-of-pocket cost for college.

Depending on the age of your children, begin structuring a plan so they can attend the colleges that meet their goals. If your children are in high school, look up their GPA's and know how many AP classes they have taken and will take in the future. Start a folder to hold any awards, certificates, essays or the report from that special project that won second place in the regional competition.

Map out a schedule for college visits during their junior year, while college is in session so the colleges that are the best fit for the student can make it to the top of the list. Most importantly, ensure your children stay on track with the myriad of deadlines that will come their way.

It may be helpful to set up a document with deadlines for PSAT, ACT/SAT test and registration dates, FAFSA priority filing deadlines for the colleges on your list, application deadlines, housing deposit deadlines, etc. Check if any of the schools on your list require the CSS Profile form or supplemental financial aid forms and ensure they are submitted by the deadline.

I've Set Up My Plan, Now What?

You have set up your basic strategy and you have assembled all your financial information, now what? You need to calculate your expected out-of-pocket cost for college, but this is very difficult to do on your own. It may take hours of research to find all the information necessary to track down the gifting levels of the colleges. EFC calculators are quite common on the Internet, but the vast majority of them are incomplete or contain outdated formulas so their accuracy is questionable.

Your best approach is probably to find a Certified College Planner in your area who can assemble an accurate estimate of where you stand in relation to your total cost of college. Most families spend more time planning vacations than planning for college, so you will most certainly end up with a better plan if you seek professional help than if you go it alone.

When seeking a professional college planner, treat it just like you would if you were changing doctors or auto mechanics. Interview the college planner, paying careful attention to what services you receive and at what price. Fees vary widely in this field. Some planners will charge you a lump sum for the entire package of services; some will charge you à la carte.

A qualified college planner will not be limited to only showing you what your expected cost of college will be based on your current situation. You should be able to find someone who will be able to provide you with a strategy customized for your family and help you lower your out-of-pocket cost substantially. Your results will improve if you can find a college planner with a background as a financial advisor because he or she will be able to ensure your college strategy is in alignment with your retirement strategies and does not reduce your income during retirement.

Remember, you use professionals to handle the important decisions of your life, including auto, life and health insurance, financial planning, mortgages, taxes and more. Consider using a professional to help you with what could be the most expensive decision of your lifetime.

If this is already overwhelming enough, to help you get the ball rolling our company, Education Planning Resources, has partnered with and trained many certified college planning specialists around the country. In order to help you decide how much opportunity you may have with your college situation, we have assembled a college evaluation to help you determine the opportunity your family may have.

You can visit www.FAFSACheck.com where you will find an opportunity to complete a free evaluation of your college cost and goals for your family. In appreciation for reading this book, you will receive one free year of college planning.

After you complete the form, you will receive an instant evaluation of your EFC and an estimate of the amount of money you may be able to save on college by adjusting to a different strategy. You will also be given the opportunity to meet with a Certified College Planner who is capable of helping your family with any of the changes that need to be made. We hope you have enjoyed reading this book and wish you the best in setting your plans for college and helping your children achieve their college dreams.

About the Authors

Stan Targosz and Will Alford started Education Planning Resources (EPR, www.EducationPlanningResources.com) to help families with all aspects of college and education planning. EPR has helped thousands of families and trained hundreds of advisors all around the country to help guide parents and students across the college mine field. In addition to leading EPR, Stan and Will host a weekly radio show, *The College Connection*, on WMUZ-FM.

Stan Targosz

Stanley (Stan) J. Targosz III has a degree from Michigan State University, is a high school graduate of Detroit Catholic Central, has been a business owner for over 20 years and has been very active in the communities that he lives and works in.

Over the past several years, Stan has worked with hundreds of families from public and private high schools. He has assisted families of all economic backgrounds. As a Senior College Planning Specialist, Stan has established himself as an expert who helps families navigate the college experience. He enjoys opening doors of opportunity to families that previously may not have known existed, helping them attend the best possible school for their children, regardless of price. He has committed himself to the education of those who want to secure a future for their children. Applied knowledge is power.

Will Alford

William (Will) H. Alford began his career as a chemist. Being recognized by his peers, and being awarded several U.S. Patents for his technical expertise helps him understand the complex formulas for the FAFSA process. Will's natural ability to take complex items and simplify them for the average person is one of the attributes that has accelerated the EPR college planning model.

Will maintains an in-depth understanding of the financial aid process, including FAFSA and Profile applications. He knows how to implement strategies that help reduce the out-of-pocket costs for parents whether their children are pursuing local, out-of-state or private universities. With his years of experience as a Senior College Planning Specialist, he has established lasting relationships with the hundreds of families he has worked with, and has a sincere appreciation for helping them accomplish their goals.

Learn More and Connect with Stan and Will:

Online: www.EducationPlanningResources.com

Email: College@EPR123.com

 LinkedIn: in/StanTargosz
              in/WillAlford

Facebook: @EducationPlanningResources

Twitter: @CollegePlan_EPR

Instagram: @CollegePlan_EPR

35932798R00095

Made in the USA
Middletown, DE
09 February 2019